P9-BVM-289

The Seeker's Guide to Being Catholic

The
Seeker's
Guide
to
Being
Catholic

MITCH FINLEY

Seeker Series

Loyola Press

CHICAGO

© 1997 Mitch Finley
All rights reserved
Printed in the United States of America

Loyola Press Seeker Series
Loyola Press
3441 North Ashland Avenue
Chicago, Illinois 60657

> **The Seeker Series** *from Loyola Press provides trustworthy guides for your journey of faith and is dedicated to the principle that asking questions is not only all right . . . it is essential.*

Series Editor: Jeremy Langford
Cover and interior design: Shawn Biner

Library of Congress Cataloging-in-Publication Data
Finley, Mitch.
The seeker's guide to being Catholic/Mitch Finley.
    p. cm. — (Seeker series)
  Includes index.
  ISBN 0-8294-0934-3
  1. Catholic Church—Apologetic works. 2. Catholic
Church—Doctrines. I. Title. II. Series.
BX1752.F563 1996
282–dc21   96-47164
                                                  CIP

1 2 3 4 5 / 01 00 99 98 97

Contents

"The desire for God is written in the human heart, because man is created by God and for God; and God never ceases to draw man to himself."

Catechism of the Catholic Church
(no. 27)

ACKNOWLEDGMENTS

My thanks to Jeremy Langford, of Loyola Press, for inviting me to write this book. Your patience, encouragement, and confidence are greatly appreciated. Thanks, also, to my sister-in-law, Terry Harvey, for perusing the Introduction and for encouragement.

All quotations from Scripture are from the New Revised Standard Version Bible: Catholic Edition, Copyright 1993 and 1989, Division of Christian Education of the National Council of Churches of Christ in the United States of America.

To Be Catholic Is To Be a Seeker

There was a time, not many decades ago, when to be Catholic was to have all the answers—at least that was the impression Catholics gave. Children learned about being Catholic from *The Baltimore Catechism*, a collection of 299 questions and answers. Once you had all the answers memorized, that meant you possessed all the basic information you needed. You had all the answers, so there was no further need to ask questions, have doubts, or look elsewhere for further information. If you did come up with a question or doubt, all you had to do was read the latest writings of the pope, or wait for the appearance of the next Vatican publication, and your question would, no doubt, receive an answer. You had it all, my friend, in a neat little package tied up with a bow.

There are some perfectly understandable reasons this situation existed, of course. It's the easiest thing in the world to look back and scoff. The church was dealing with a nation of poorly educated immigrants, for example, for whom the old catechism was ideally suited. It did its job well for its time and place. Still, the situation has changed.

Catholics no longer inhabit such a spiritually secure world. Being Catholic today means being a seeker, a pilgrim, a person with questions, doubts, and insecurities. Most Catholics no longer think of the Vatican as an answer machine and their faith as a security blanket. Rather, to be Catholic is to embrace a faith that sometimes requires you to take chances and stick your neck out. Faith is a source of security only, by analogy, in the way that a relationship with another human being is a source of security. You never know where a relationship will take you or what it will demand of you.

The *Catechism of the Catholic Church* puts it this way: "Faith is a personal act—the free response of the human person to the initiative of God who reveals himself" (no. 166).

Apply this description of faith to the relationship between husband and wife, or between two close friends, and you will have a good idea of what it means. Just as in a marriage or friendship we respond to the other who reveals himself or herself, in faith we respond to God's self-revelation in creation, in ourselves, in our relationships, and in our other experiences. Just as in a marriage or friendship we say yes to the other's self-revelation through his or her deeds and words, so in faith we do the same with God.

Such an understanding of faith includes living with insecurity, not having all the answers, but being ready to trust and hope all the same. Faith is more of an adventure than a security blanket. Faith is more of a pilgrimage than a cozy, secure little nook by the fireplace — although sometimes it can be that, as well. Faith is both a challenge and a comfort, usually in an unpredictable manner.

Some people think of religion as a crutch for those who aren't strong enough to face life on their own. Flannery O'Connor (1925–1964) was a Catholic and the first woman author to be included in the prestigious Library of America series. In her posthumous collection of letters, *The Habit of Being* (Farrar, Straus & Giroux, 1979, p.), Flannery O'Connor wrote an excellent response to the charge that religion is a crutch for the weak:

> What people don't realize is how much religion costs. They think faith is a big electric blanket, when of course it is the cross. It is much harder to believe than not to believe. . . .
>
> Don't expect faith to clear things up for you. It is trust, not certainty. . .

These words are as Catholic as they can be, and they deserve to be taken seriously. "It is much harder to believe than not to believe." For Catholicism, faith is an act of courage, and it is not easy. Sometimes being Catholic can be frustrating and difficult. But most Catholics remain Catholic because they find in Catholicism such a deep source of joy, courage, enlightenment and freedom, because they find there "grace upon grace" (John 1:16). A Catholic—one who is Catholic in his or her heart—is someone who values freedom over security, trust over certainty.

We live in an era when religion has a bad name with a great many people, those who buy into a secularized world view and believe that to live with no connections to "organized religion" is an act of strength and courage. As Flannery O'Connor suggested, of course, the choice to live a secularized life may be the easier option. There is far more cultural support for not being Catholic than for being Catholic. No one will make fun of you for not being Catholic. Most people in our society will not criticize you for not attending Mass on Sunday, neither will anyone compliment you for doing so. If anything, others will nod approvingly if you announce that you are an ex-Catholic. As far as the dominant popular culture is concerned, it's understandable if you were "raised Catholic," but only a fool would cling to all that nonsense past the age of eighteen, much less convert to it as an adult.

It's also true, of course, that many people in our society embrace sectarian forms of Christianity that offer absolute certainty about all of life's most difficult questions. Indeed, some Catholics cling to an interpretation of Catholicism that offers the same kind of certainty. Still others are attracted to non-Christian religions, eastern forms of mysticism, New Age religions, or they fashion a private, personalized, eclectic "spirituality" that has nothing to do with "organized religion" and little if anything to do with membership in a community. For many people it's acceptable to have a "spirituality," but "institutional religion" is a horror you must avoid if you want true freedom of spirit.

If you are uncomfortable with the popular perspective that requires you to have no faith or think of religion as a mere hobby that has nothing to do with the real world; if you are dissatisfied with fashioning a private, "mixed bag" spirituality designed to satisfy personal needs but make few demands; if you cannot agree with the sectarian Christian perspective that requires you to turn off your intellect and embrace blind faith in exchange for absolute certainty; if you believe that Catholicism, the oldest institution in the western world, is not perfect, but it may have something to offer all the same—this book is for you.

The purpose of this small book is to offer some tips, some guidelines, on being a Catholic seeker. Perhaps you are curious about Catholicism, or you are thinking of becoming a Catholic. Maybe you were raised in Catholicism but you don't know if it fits into your future or not. Or, maybe you are Catholic and simply want to know more about what that means in today's complex, sometimes confusing world. This book will not answer all your questions, but it will join you in asking those questions and thinking about some possible responses. Think of this book as a literary companion on your quest.

Being Catholic is not a part-time hobby and the Catholic Church is not a civic or fraternal organization. Being Catholic is not something you do in your spare time; attending Mass on

Sundays is not like going to the meetings of a club. Catholicism is a way of life, and the church is a people, a community you belong to much as one belongs to a family, with all the ups and downs, joys and frustrations of family life. Being Catholic can make you "crazy" sometimes; it's not unusual for Catholics to sometimes be frustrated, even angry, at their church — which is to say their community, their leaders, and their institutions. More often, if you take the trouble to find out what being Catholic is *really* all about, being Catholic can make you more sane, and more honest, than you have ever been before. Being Catholic is not something you *do*, it's something you *are*.

This book does not pretend to be a complete presentation of the Catholic faith. The *Catechism of the Catholic Church* (Libreria Editrice Vaticana, 1994) is the official version of that kind of book, and sooner or later you may find it advantageous to own a copy. *Catholicism*, New Revised Edition, by Father Richard P. McBrien (HarperSanFrancisco, 1994), is an unofficial but excellent version of that same, all-encompassing kind of book.

The slim volume you hold in your hands can only serve as a sparkplug, something to ignite you to go on seeking, to stay faithful to your quest for loving intimacy with your Creator, an intimacy characterized by truth, freedom, and deep joy. The author is one who loves being Catholic, one who sometimes finds the church a source of "craziness," but one who believes that there is more to be said *for* being Catholic than for *not* being Catholic. The author, in other words, believes that to be Catholic is to be a seeker. He is a fairly typical Catholic who wouldn't be anything else. Ever.

May this book be for you a blessing.

The author of this book is sensitive to the need for gender inclusive language, particularly when referring to human beings. Vatican officials who author official church documents (that is, the *Cathechism of the Catholic Church* and papal encyclicals) do not yet share this sensitivity. So it goes.

The reader will discover that in this book the author makes no attempt to conceal or gloss over the church's "shadow side," and this includes the Vatican's apparent insensitivity to the impact on English-speaking readers of noninclusive terminology. The author believes that there is no malice on the part of Vatican officials who do this, and it seemed artificial to insert corrective words and phrases in brackets at every turn.

When a quotation from an official church document uses what strikes the reader as non-inclusive language, such as "man" or "he," be patient; remember that the intention of the authors is inclusive whether it strikes us that way or not. "Man" means "humankind" or "people," and exclusively masculine pronouns are a side effect of traditional language. With time and patience the problem will be corrected.

"In Christian usage, the word 'church' designates the liturgical assembly, but also the local community or the whole universal community of believers. These three meanings are inseparable."

Catechism of the Catholic Church

(no. 752)

The Heart of
the Matter

Did you ever wonder what being Catholic, rock bottom, is all about? Did you ever wonder what the church, and all the church's doctrines, traditions, and institutions boil down to? Did you ever want to clear away all that's not essential and get to the heart of what it means to be a Catholic?

In this first chapter, we will throw around some ideas about this; your task will be to reflect on what you read here and see how it resonates with your own experience. In a very real sense, this chapter lays a foundation for the rest of the book, which will then "unpack" the basic ideas set forth here.

It's understandable that anyone with an inquiring mind, on a seeker's journey, may want to get down to brass tacks. Sometimes the

church can seem weighed down with centuries-old traditions, obscure theological
debates, church politics, scandals now and
then, and the conflicts that occasionally
develop in parish life. Today, especially, the
church often seems to be filled with in-fight-
ing—liberals and conservatives condemning
one another, various factions hurling verbal
barbs. It can seem downright sad. Why must
there be so much squabbling over what it
means to be "a good Catholic"? Why can't we
set our differences aside and get on with it?

One important reply to this question comes
from G. K. Chesterton (1874–1936), one of the
most-quoted, English-speaking Catholics of
the twentieth century. He said: "Catholics
know the two or three transcendental truths on
which they do agree; and take rather a pleasure
in disagreeing on everything else."

In other words, there are only a few essential truths at the heart of the Catholic faith, and
almost no one disagrees about these. The
Apostles' Creed is an ancient Christian summary of these essential beliefs:

> I believe in God, the Father almighty,
> creator of heaven and earth. I believe in
> Jesus Christ, his only son, our Lord. He
> was conceived by the power of the Holy
> Spirit and born of the Virgin Mary. He

suffered under Pontius Pilate, was crucified, died and was buried. On the third day
he rose again. He ascended into heaven,
and is seated at the right hand of the
Father. He will come to judge the living
and the dead. I believe in the Holy Spirit,
the holy catholic church, the communion of
saints, the forgiveness of sins, the resurrection of the body, and life everlasting. Amen.

Notice in passing, the Apostles' Creed, like
other traditional formulations of faith and
prayers, is loaded with metaphors because all
religious language is metaphorical. God is not
literally a Father, but "Father" is a scriptural
metaphor Jesus used to communicate an idea
of God as a loving Papa. When the creed states
that Jesus "rose again" and "ascended into
heaven" these are what we might call "action
metaphors" that describe a real event that happened in history yet transcends history. Such
metaphors communicate truth, but in a limited
fashion. They are much better than nothing.
All such language is an attempt to express and
talk about human experience of divine realities,
and human language can never fully express
what we're talking about. On the one hand, we
can't take metaphors literally. On the other
hand, metaphors are all we have, so we can't do
without them. If we are open to our metaphors

precisely *as metaphors* they can touch the heart and enlighten the mind. If we take them literally, however, they can lead to trouble. In a sense, what we need to do is *look through* the metaphors, or allow the divine to shine through them. A religious metaphor is meant to be like a window, not like a statement of scientific fact etched in stone.

Back to our main line of thought, however: The issues and concerns Catholics "take rather a pleasure in disagreeing on" are significant but, when push comes to shove, they are not the heart of the matter. Catholics may disagree about how the Mass should be structured, about the meaning of one of Jesus' parables in the Gospels, or about the best way to respond to a contemporary social, political, or economic issue. Catholics may—and do!—disagree about the use of artificial contraceptives, about divorce, or about capital punishment. All of these issues are important, but they are not absolutely foundational to what it means to be a Catholic.

Catholics may even disagree with an official church teaching and still be "good Catholics." Being a "good Catholic" means, ultimately, following one's conscience. "Everyone is obliged to follow a sincerely informed conscience," writes Father Philip S. Kauffman, O.S.B., in *Why You Can Disagree and Remain a*

Faithful Catholic, New Revised and Expanded Edition (Crossroad Publishing Co., 1995). "This definitely does not mean that we do whatever we please. It does mean that once we have made an honest effort to determine what we should do or avoid doing, we have an obligation to act according to that conviction."

More about this, however, in Chapter 9 . . .

The trouble, of course, is that sometimes those who disagree forget that what they disagree about is of secondary importance. They act as if their disagreement about the liturgy, some official church teaching, or a fine theological point is absolutely basic when, in fact, it is not. A moment's reflection reveals that the argument at hand concerns something about which there may never be a Catholic consensus. But we sure "get into" arguing about it!

If we think of the church as a big family, we should not be surprised that so many arguments and disagreements take place. What family does not witness conflict among its members? Another of Chesterton's observations—this one about the family in his *Heretics* (1950)—applies equally well to the church:

> Of course the family [read: "the church"] is a good institution because it is uncongenial. It is wholesome precisely

because it contains so many divergences and varieties. It is . . . like a little kingdom, and, like most other little kingdoms . . . generally in a state of something resembling anarchy. . . . Aunt Elizabeth is unreasonable, like mankind. Papa is excitable, like mankind. Our youngest brother is mischievous, like mankind. Grandpapa is stupid, like the world; he is old, like the world.

The church "is wholesome precisely because it contains so many divergences and varieties." We sometimes forget that all the wrangling and fussing that goes on in the church is a *sign of life.* If the church were a dying institution no one would care enough to argue about it. But because it is alive—indeed, going through the labor pains of coming to a new birth—the signs of life are rampant.

Because the church is alive the pastor is unreasonable ("like mankind"). Because Catholicism is vibrant and its people filled with hope, sometimes they say that the bishop is stupid ("like the world"). Because the Catholic faith holds so much promise for the future, sometimes Catholics complain that the church is old ("like the world").

What is the heart of the matter, the essence of Catholicism? The answer to this question is simple yet laden with mystery. The heart of the matter is our ongoing experience of Jesus the risen Christ. That's what any form of Christian faith is about. But this statement leads to endless implications, questions, debates, and disagreements — "divergences and varieties." Otherwise there would not be so many perspectives on what it means to be a true follower of Christ and a "good Catholic."

So once again we pose the question, but this time in a different way. What determines whether one is a Catholic or not? This is the question of orthodoxy, the question about what is true to the accepted, traditional Catholic faith. Theologian Father Richard McBrien, from the University of Notre Dame, outlined "the limits of orthodoxy." In his nationally syndicated newspaper column, he insisted that there are limits beyond which one is no longer a Catholic.

For example, Father McBrien explained, Catholics believe in the reality of God — the Divine Mystery, the Supernatural, the Holy, the Transcendent One. At the same time, Catholics believe that God has a triune nature — in traditional terms that God is Father, Son, and Holy Spirit while still one Person. Notice that we are back in the thick of metaphors. "Person" is a metaphor for a reality our puny intellects can never hope to grasp. Its purpose is to announce that God is not a cold, impersonal "life force" but Unconditional Love.

God is not the philosophers' indifferent "ground of all being." Rather, God is "personal" and relates to us in a loving, caring, personal way. Indeed, God's love for us, as individuals and in relationship with one another, is unconditional, passionate, and absolutely reliable. Karl Rahner, S.J., probably the greatest Catholic theologian of the twentieth century, said that all his vast and profound theological reflections could be summed up in one simple statement: "God dwells in you." Even in the dark face of suffering and death Catholics believe that this is true.

Catholics believe that the triune God created us and all that exists ("Father"), redeemed us ("Son"), and makes us holy ("Holy Spirit")—and another way to say "holy" is "hale and hearty." Catholics believe that Father, Son, and Holy Spirit—three in one— guide us through our own exercise of human freedom toward the final Reign, or Kingdom, of God. This means that ultimately God's loving presence will permeate everything that exists. Notice, again, that as we move along, metaphors for God are rampant, for they are all we have to talk about the Divine Mystery.

Catholics believe that Jesus the Christ is a divine Person with both a fully human and a fully divine nature. Catholics believe that Jesus redeemed us by his loving acceptance of death on the cross and by his Resurrection. This is what we mean by "salvation," a term that denotes spiritual healing and liberation. "Resurrection," too, is a metaphor for an actual historical event that leaves the human intellect in its dust but also fills us with hope, joy, and new life.

Catholics believe that human nature is fallen—flawed or disordered. But we also believe that we are "redeemed" or "saved," and that grace—God's self-gift to us—is more powerful than sin and guilt. Catholics believe that salvation—spiritual liberation and healing—is the gift of God and that human freedom is required to accept or reject that gift.

Catholics believe that the church, which means all of us, the people of God, is more than a human organization or community, that it is a mystery, a human reality saturated with the hidden presence of God. Still, the church's glorious humanity and sometimes tragic imperfections cannot be denied. Back in the 1940s, a great Italian-born German theologian, Romano Guardini, expressed this truth in a startling manner. He said that the church is the cross that Christ was crucified on.

It would be childish to expect the church to measure up to our standards of perfection. The church is an imperfect, sometimes even sinful human institution. But it is also where we find the deepest well of God's healing love and the most reliable light by which to live our lives.

Remember, the Catholic Church is the oldest institution in the western world. The church tends to move slowly, and sometimes it doesn't see things as clearly as it might. What's amazing about the church is not that its vision is sometimes clouded but that it sees so clearly so much of the time.

Catholics believe in the spiritual effectiveness of the seven sacraments — Baptism, Confirmation, Eucharist, Reconciliation, Marriage, Holy Orders, and Anointing of the Sick — and that these sacraments are signs and instruments of Christ's saving activity on our behalf. In the sacraments we experience in a special, unique way the presence and activity of the risen Christ. In the sacraments the risen Christ touches us in the ways we most need to be touched.

Catholics believe that the whole person — "body and blood, soul and divinity" — of the risen Christ is sacramentally present in the bread and wine consecrated at Mass. The risen Christ is present first of all in the community gathered for Mass, in the priest who presides at Mass, then — and most specially — in the consecrated bread and wine.

Catholics believe in the forgiveness of sins, the resurrection of the body, and eternal life. At the same time, Catholics don't claim to have a complete understanding of the realities that these words refer to. We're talking about profound and holy mysteries here, not a recipe for a spiritual entree or step-by-step directions for how to be "saved."

Notice that this outline of what constitutes "orthodoxy" leaves much room for serious, deeply thought-out differences of opinion, even disagreements with some official church teachings. It's not unusual for this to happen. For example, the *Catechism of the Catholic Church* is not equal to the Bible, it's more like "tips and guidelines"—very special tips and guidelines, to be sure, deserving of deep respect, but tips and guidelines all the same, subject to revisions and reformulations as time goes by. In fact, this has already happened. Within a couple of years after the publication of the new catechism, the Vatican announced that a subsequent edition of the catechism would include the previously absent declaration that capital punishment is contrary to Catholic faith.

We're not talking automatic infallibility every time the pope or a Vatican agency lets drop with a teaching. As Pope John XXIII said during the early 1960s: "Authentic doctrine has to be studied and expounded in the light of the research methods and the language of modern thought. For the substance of the ancient deposit of faith is one thing, and the way in which it is presented is another."

Father McBrien's summary of what it means to be an orthodox Catholic is incomplete and has its limits. What he says is perfectly true, but he confined his remarks to Catholic doctrines, and doctrines have no life if separated from their source. The ultimate source of Catholic doctrines is Catholic life, and Catholic life is rooted in the faith community's ongoing experience of the risen Christ in its midst for some two thousand years now.

The heart of the Catholic matter is a way of life, a way of life rooted in our—the church's—centuries-old, ongoing, loving intimacy with the risen Christ, including all the forms it has taken and all it has given rise to. Another name for this experience is Sacred Tradition. It was Sacred Tradition that gave birth to the Christian Scriptures or New Testament. It was the first-century Christian communities' shared memories of the historical Jesus and their experience of the risen Christ in their midst, in various social, political, and cultural circumstances, that gave birth to the New Testament, and it is in the New Testament that we find the standards according to which we measure ourselves and our lives.

The various New Testament documents together form the primary guide for our way of life as Catholic Christians. But they do so in the midst of and rooted in our ongoing experience of Sacred Tradition, the same experience of the risen Christ that gave birth to the New Testament in the first place. That's why it is so important that we read and interpret the New Testament *as a faith community*, not merely as isolated individuals.

People who interpret the New Testament in isolation from the community of faith sometimes get crackpot ideas and do crackpot things. One reason is that such people are out of touch with the Sacred Tradition, living and active in the church/faith community today, from which the New Testament emerged in the first place.

"Sacred Tradition and Sacred Scripture, then, are bound closely together and communicate one with the other. For both of them, flowing out from the same divine well-spring, come together in some fashion to form one thing and move towards the same goal. Each of them makes present and fruitful in the Church the mystery of Christ, who promised to remain with his own 'always, to the close of the age' [Matthew 28:20]" (*Catechism of the Catholic Church,* no. 80).

As a community of faith, Catholics find themselves inspired and guided by both the

Scriptures and Sacred Tradition. We find ourselves inspired and guided by the risen Christ in our midst to live a life based on love of God and loving service to other people, particularly our "neighbors," those with whom we live and work most closely. But we do this in a world that sometimes has little sympathy for such a project.

In other words, the Catholic Christian way of life is countercultural. This is not to say that Catholics try to be as weird as possible at every opportunity. Catholics see no sense in being different for the sake of being different. It simply means that because we take love of God and neighbor as the basis for a life worth living, we sometimes find ourselves going against the grain, swimming upstream, in conflict with some of the values, standards, and ideals that the dominant culture takes for granted. Therefore, there are times when we look different and live a different way.

To be Catholic means embracing a way of life and a spirituality that takes love of God and loving service of other people as its ultimate standard. This means that in everything we are, and everything we do, we ask ourselves questions like these: "How does what I am doing help me to love God and neighbor? How am I, as a unique person, called to live a life that expresses love of God and neighbor?"

If we are honest about our responses to these questions we will find ourselves making choices focussed not on self but on God and other people. It's as simple, and profound, as that.

To speak of "love," however, is a risky business. Our culture uses the word "love" in superficial ways sometimes. When Catholicism uses the word "love" it uses it first in the way that Jesus did, and when Catholicism looks for an example of love's deepest meaning it discovers it first in the image and example of Jesus. In the Gospel of John, Jesus says: "No one has greater love than this, to lay down one's life for one's friends" (15:13).

There is nothing superficial about this understanding of love. The great Russian novelist Fyodor Dostoevsky (1821–81) said it another way in *The Brothers Karamazov*. The monk Zossima declares that "active love is a harsh and fearful thing compared with love in dreams."

The heart of the Catholic matter is love, but it is a love that does not depend on the feelings of the moment or dreamy romanticism. Important as our emotions are, the love at the heart of a Catholic life is a love that is fundamentally an act of the will. It does not depend on emotional rewards to go on loving. Saint Thomas Aquinas (c. 1225–74), probably the most influential Catholic theologian of all time, said in the thirteenth century that to love means "to will the good of the other."

This is the kind of love that makes marriages successful, that keeps parents faithful to their children, that keeps single adults rooted in a life inspired and guided by faith, that anchors a priest in his vocation and keeps monks and nuns who live in monasteries dedicated to their life of prayer and manual labor. This is the kind of love that Jesus lived and the risen Christ inspires today. This is the love that is at the heart of what it means to be Catholic.

Clear away all the secondary stuff, and in Catholicism you find a centuries-old religious tradition based on love of God and neighbor, a love with divine steel at its center, a love that cherishes life in all its forms and in all its stages. Catholicism says that life is at its fullest only when it is founded on and dedicated to living this kind of love.

This isn't all we find at the heart of Catholicism, however. Catholics not only dedicate themselves to a life of active love, they also have a unique vision of life and the world. Listen. This is a great mystery. Catholics find God—"the Love that moves the sun and the other stars," to quote Dante's *Divine Comedy*— around every corner, under every leaf, behind every door and in every sunset and every rising of the moon. Everything in creation is "like" God or reflects God's love.

In other words, Catholics milk some words of Saint Paul for all they are worth: "Ever since the creation of the world [God's] eternal power and divine nature, invisible though they are, have been understood and seen through the things he has made" (Romans 1:20).

This is a thoroughly Catholic characteristic. Classical Protestantism has a different vision of life and the world, one which emphasizes the divine *absence* from creation rather than the divine presence, how *different* God is from all that is human and all that is in creation. The Protestant perspective has truth about it, too. To be sure. There is plenty of darkness in the world. But Catholicism prefers to emphasize God's presence rather than God's absence. Catholics find reminders of God's loving intimacy with people and all of creation here, there, and everywhere.

At the heart of Catholicism there are two cornerstones, if you will. One is a way of life founded on the entrance of the Son of God into human history and his teaching that the meaning of life is found in love of God and neighbor. The other is a constant vision of life and the world that emphasizes God's love present in the world and finds God's glory in countless places, public and private. This is what Catholicism is about with all the incidentals stripped away, and everything else builds on these two cornerstones.

"Incorporated into Christ by Baptism, Christians are 'dead to sin and alive to God in Christ Jesus' [Romans 6:11] and so participate in the life of the Risen Lord. Following Christ and united with him, Christians can strive to be 'imitators of God as beloved children, and walk in love' [Ephesians 5:1–2] by conforming their thoughts, words and actions to the 'mind . . . which is yours in Christ Jesus' [Philippians 2:5], and by following his example."

Catechism of the Catholic Church
(no. 1694)

Life Choices Vocation

As a seeker, one question uppermost in your mind may be the question of vocation. We're not talking about the work or career you choose. We will address that topic in the next chapter. Rather, we're talking about your most basic life commitment, the way in which you express your baptismal promise to live a life dedicated to God and neighbor.

What way of life am I called by God to embrace? What does God want me to do with my life? Am I meant to marry and have a family? Am I best suited to remain single? Does God want me to become a priest, join a religious community, or enter a monastery, perhaps become a permanent deacon? This is a wonderful question to face, a question that leads you on an adventure, a quest, a trek into the future. At the same time, it isn't an easy question to answer, not for most people, at least.

Sometimes we have the idea that God wants us to do something but it's hidden, and it's our job to figure out the secret. From this perspective, we would spend much time asking God to let us know what to do with our lives. "I wish I could figure out God's will for me." But God is not forthcoming with the information, not in any obvious fashion. There is no such thing as e-mail from God.

This approach seems to presume an understanding of God that is rather small. Keep in mind that "God" is simply a word we use to talk about the Divine Mystery. "God" is the word we use to remind ourselves that at the roots of our being we are intimately related to a personal reality that is, all the same, completely different from the limited things of this world. We use the word "God" to talk about the Love that holds each one of us, and the entire universe, in existence, a Love that is way beyond our ability to think about it.

This approach also overlooks the fact that we are free, and God—the Divine Mystery who is Unconditional Love at the roots of our being—wants us to exercise our freedom by making choices. It also overlooks the fact that

God gives each person gifts, talents, inclinations, and a unique temperament and personality. By working with these, we work with God's will for us. In other words, there are two wills active here, God's and ours. We make the best choices we can, in a prayerful manner, and God works with those choices. "We know that all things work together for good for those who love God . . ." (Romans 8:28).

We discover God's will by following our own interests, enthusiasms, and what touches us most deeply. In this sense, the famous mythologist Joseph Campbell (1904–87) offered good advice when he said, "Follow your bliss." I discover my special vocation from God not as a treasure locked in a box that I must find the key for. Rather, I find my vocation by following my own best and most noble inclinations, by prayerful openness to being guided by the Holy Spirit, and by preparing myself for the unexpected.

At the same time, it's critically important to keep in mind that for all the satisfaction we may gain from our vocation, any Christian vocation is a calling to love, and love is never authentic unless we give it away. Ponder some words of the great Trappist monk, spiritual master, and author, Thomas Merton (1915–68), in his 1955 classic, *No Man Is an Island*:

A happiness that is sought for ourselves alone can never be found: for a happiness that is diminished by being shared is not big enough to make us happy.

There is a false and momentary happiness in self-satisfaction, but it always leads to sorrow because it narrows and deadens our spirit. True happiness is found in unselfish love, a love which increases in proportion as it is shared. There is no end to the sharing of love, and, therefore, the potential happiness of such love is without limit. Infinite sharing is the law of God's inner life. He has made the sharing of ourselves the law of our own being, so that it is in loving others that we best love ourselves. In disinterested activity we best fulfill our own capacities to act and to be.

Sometimes God's will comes as a complete surprise, catching us off-guard. Only in retrospect do we see that, by golly, God's love was there all along preparing us and our way into the future. One of the most obvious and common examples is when a young man and woman meet, fall in love, and decide to marry. Perhaps neither expected to find someone who could share his or her deepest values, beliefs, and enthusiasms. But it happened all the same, and it came as a surprise to them both. They discovered God's will and vocation for them, when they least expected it. It happens all the time.

Quite often we uncover our vocation gradually, over a number of years. Sometimes we discover our vocation, and maybe on the surface, at least, we're not that crazy about the idea. This may happen in the case of a vocation to the priesthood or religious life. Reluctance to accept such a vocation can be a sign that this is, in fact, your vocation. Initially, at least, reluctance to become a priest or religious may be a healthy sign. Someone who has a huge enthusiasm for becoming a priest or religious should examine his or her motives carefully. Am I excited about this idea because I like the thought of the power or influence that comes with being a priest or religious? Are my motives self- or other-centered?

One of the best signs of a vocation from God is its refusal to go away. If the idea of being married, or becoming a priest or religious, keeps nagging at you, won't leave you alone, chances are good that this is your vocation and you had better get cracking. Sometimes, of course, we may feel a deep desire for marriage and family life but no prospective spouse comes along. In this case, it can be a major, big-time mistake to marry the first willing person. A vocation to marriage means marrying the *right* person, not just whoever turns up and is ready to say, "I do." Of course, it's also true that any number of people could be "right" for you.

The key to marrying well, or becoming a good priest or good religious, is the same no matter what your vocation may be. The key is to grow up, plain and simple. We can't discover our true vocation in life until we have a good idea of who we are, what we believe, what our deepest values are, and what we believe is the most basic purpose of life. One of the best set of questions for any seeker to reflect upon is this: "What do you think is the purpose of life? What would you be willing to die for? Better yet, what are you willing to *live* for? What do you want out of life, more than anything else?"

The answers we give to questions like these reveal who we are, our deepest values, and our deepest beliefs about the meaning of life. From a Christian point of view, our replies to these questions need to be connected in some way with the heart of Jesus' teaching that any life finds its deepest meaning in love of God and neighbor. If we honestly believe that the purpose of life is to become as comfortable and secure as possible, and never take any risks, then we are distant from a Christian way of life. In this case our quest for our true vocation is bound to run off the road and into the ditch. Once we have our priorities straight, with a life dedicated to God and neighbor as our basic goal, then our vocation will reveal itself in good time.

Most people are called to marriage and family life. But in our time, at least, many seem called to remain single. A single life is not an incomplete life by any means. It is a vocation with its own rewards, challenges, and missions. Perhaps the most prominent characteristic of a vocation to a single life is flexibility. Whereas married people and parents find themselves with many commitments and demands on their time that are "built in," a single person must constantly make decisions about the use of his or her time and other resources.

True story: Maria, a twenty-something college graduate with a good career in public relations, found herself more and more dissatisfied with her work. The stress level was high, and she found it necessary to work long hours. "It was like my whole life was taken up by my job," she later recalled. "It was crazy."

Each Sunday at Mass, Maria began praying for guidance. What should she do to get her life under control? With the help of a friend who served as a wise spiritual guide, over several months Maria decided to leave her lucrative but stressful job in public relations and become a volunteer lay missionary in South

America. For two years she lived in a culture foreign to her. "It was among very poor people that I learned the real meaning and purpose of life," Maria said. "But I never could have done that unless I had been single. Being single gave me the freedom to have experiences none of my married friends with children could have."

When Maria returned to the United States she again pursued her career in public relations, but she did so determined to retain control of her life. "I found a position with a small firm in a relatively small city," she said, "and the owners have a social conscience. For example, we do a certain amount of work at a reduced rate, or sometimes free, for churches and social service agencies.

"I don't make as much money as I did before, but I don't miss the money because I prefer a simpler lifestyle now. Also, I have so much more time to myself, time to do other things, to relax, to be with other people, to be involved in my parish, even some time to do volunteer work at a school for kids with developmental disabilities. I like my life a lot right now. I may get married some day, but I'm in no hurry. I'm leaving that in God's hands. I have a full, balanced life right now, a life that I'm grateful for because I'm not centered on myself, I'm centered on others."

Eventually most people do marry and have families, and when they do they find a built-in orientation to living for God and others. Marriage is a shift in lifestyle and a shift in spirituality. People who get married thinking they can go on living as they did when single have a rude awakening coming to them. Marriage is a vocation, a calling, which leads us into a life-for-the-other. Spouses need to always take each other into account. It is no longer possible to make decisions independently. Even minor choices such as what to do this evening or this weekend require consultation with one's spouse.

Sometimes single people worry that marriage means "giving up all my freedom." From a Catholic point of view, the deepest exercise of one's freedom happens when he or she chooses a vocation. This, of course, rules out all the other options, at least for as far as we can see into the future. It's a paradox. When we use our freedom to make a choice we find ourselves with fewer choices open to us, but because we made a free choice we now find ourselves free on a deeper level than we were before. Because I made a free choice from among all the options open to me, now my life has a clear direction, a definite shape it didn't have before. Instead of floundering about, first in this direction, then in that direction, never with a clear focus to my life, now I have a clear focus and purpose to live for. What could be more free than that?

Tom, who has been married for three years, looks back on the months prior to his wedding with a smile. "I really sweated out the whole marriage thing," he said. "I knew that I loved Tara and wanted to marry her, but I had a thing about my freedom as a single person to do whatever I wanted to, whenever I wanted to do it. It's been a real revelation to me to find that in marriage, and now being a new father, that I don't miss all that unfettered, so-called freedom. I feel more free now than I ever did before, and I think it's because now my life has a purpose that's bigger than I am, bigger than the two of us. It's good, it's really good."

Tara nods in agreement: "It's not like we're inseparably joined in a physical sense, we're not Siamese twins. We give each other time to do things alone. We each need a break from the baby now and then, and we do that for each other. But being married gives life a deeper purpose that wasn't there before, and having a baby definitely makes that even more profound."

The same is true of any vocation. To accept a calling to the priesthood or religious life gives a person's life a clear direction, and moving in that direction I find myself with other choices to make. Do I want to be a parish priest?

Belong to a religious order, such as the Jesuits or the Franciscans? Become a teacher or scholar? Even in a monastery one must use one's natural gifts and talents. One becomes an administrator, a cook, an office worker, a writer, whatever work one does best that is needed by the monastic community.

Sister Rachel decided to join a religious community in her mid-thirties after what she calls "a long career as a single person." Looking back, she sees that her life as a single person went through several phases. "After I left college," she explained, "I had a job and lived alone. For a few years I really got into having no ties, no commitments to anything or anyone. I thought that was great, but it got old. I found that making no promises leads other people to think of you as unreliable and untrustworthy. I would show up for my job, of course, because I wanted to keep it, but other than that I was footloose and fancy-free. If I didn't feel like going to Mass on Sunday I didn't go. If someone asked me to meet them at a certain time I would always be late. That kind of thing."

Sister Rachel found that her life felt empty. She experimented with drugs, but she didn't feel good about that and fortunately she got away from the drug scene before it became a serious problem. Later, when a chance came along to attend a retreat for young adults she decided to go and see what would happen. "It was a life-changing experience for me," she recalled. "I saw that a life with no commitments, no focus on others, is an empty, meaningless life. So for the next ten years or so I gave a lot of my time to helping out at a day care facility for single moms. I dated and even had a couple of serious relationships, but none of them seemed right for a lifelong commitment. Gradually, I began to think about the religious life and, well, here I am!"

Since completing her religious congregation's formation program, Sister Rachel has worked with two other Sisters on a Native American reservation in the Pacific Northwest. "This is what life is all about," she commented. "Once you make a permanent commitment to a vocation, no matter what it may be, then you go deeper into the meaning and purpose of life."

Father Joe, a recently ordained diocesan priest, is in his late twenties. He, too, speaks of the need to live for others by finding and accepting a vocation. "The priesthood is tricky terrain, especially today," he said. "There is much uncertainty about the role and place of priests in the church. The Catholic population is increasing by leaps and bounds, but the number of priests is decreasing steadily, so a priest's life is very busy, and it can be a pressure cooker situation if you don't stay in control. Some people think women and married men should be ordained, others disagree. You have all the negative publicity about pedophilia among priests—very few, really—which doesn't help our image at all. It's strange. At the same time, I think most priests are glad to be doing what they are doing, I think they're glad to be priests. I know it's a good thing for me. It's where God wants me to be."

Father Joe decided to become a priest a few years after he finished college and taught in a public high school. "The need in our society for people to do what a priest does, to be not only a leader and facilitator in a parish, but to be a public witness to the value and importance of the sacred in our world, I don't think that will go away soon. It's very rewarding, and it gives my life more depth, meaning, and purpose than it had before.

"Sure, I thought about marriage and a family, but the sacrifices the priesthood requires right now are, I think, worth it in a world where so many people think another person can make you happy, or you can buy happiness in a store. Everyone makes sacrifices when they choose a vocation; the sacrifices I make just happen to be countercultural so there isn't a lot of support for them. I happen to think that makes them all the more worth making."

A vocation—whether to be single, married, a priest or religious—is a sacred reality, a calling from God that has close connections to our natural interests and abilities. Time was, a couple of generations ago, a vocation to the priesthood or religious life was, in practice if not in theory, held up as superior to all others. Marriage was good, religious life was better, the priesthood was best—and a vocation to a single life was hardly even discussed. In fact, vocations are different but none is superior to the others. The best vocation is what's best for you.

The most effective way to find one's lifelong vocation is to live whatever vocation you find yourself with right now as deeply as you can in the spirit of the gospel. The gospel will lead you on, for it is the good news of God's unconditional love and the good news that life's deepest meaning is found in the love of God and loving service to other people. As long as we try to do this we will find our vocation . . . or rather, our vocation will find us.

"In work, the person exercises and fulfills in part the potential inscribed in his nature. The primordial value of labor stems from man himself, its author and beneficiary. Work is for man, not man for work."

Catechism of the Catholic Church
(no. 2428)

Life Choices
Work

What does work have to do with being Catholic? Work is such a big part of most people's lives that it is natural for a seeker to ask this question. What do all these hours I spend on work, day in, day out, week after week, month after month, year after year, have to do with who I am, the meaning of life, the purpose of my existence? What's the point?

In his 1981 encyclical, "On Human Work," Pope John Paul II articulated what many regard as the best modern statement of how work belongs to our most basic identity as human beings and followers of Christ. The pope explains that all persons are created in the image of God. Because we are created by God, in the image of God, we are called to live out our identity by working in and with God's creation:

The word of God's revelation is profoundly marked by the fundamental truth that man, created in the image of God, shares by his work in the activity of the creator, and that, within the limits of his own human capabilities, man in a sense continues to develop that activity and perfects it as he advances further and further in the discovery of the resources and values contained in the whole of creation (no. 25).

Work is not a punishment for sin, as some people believe. Rather, work is a blessing and a way for us to live our faith on a daily basis. We need to work in order to generate income, it's true. But work should be more than a way to pay the rent and buy the groceries.

What about this idea that work is a curse? Recall the story of Adam and Eve in the Book of Genesis. When Adam and Eve disobey God, part of what Adam hears from God is this: "By the sweat of your face you shall eat bread. . ." (3:19).

Conventional wisdom interprets this to mean that work is part of God's punishment for sin, and because we all share in the effects of the sin of Adam and Eve we also share in their punishment. This is only partly correct. Notice that the description Genesis gives of the blissful original condition in the Garden of Eden includes *work:* "The LORD God took the man and put him in the garden of Eden to till it and keep it" (2:15).

In other words, work was in the picture from the beginning; work is supposed to be a part of God's original blessing on humankind. As part of the original picture, work was integral to humanity's happy condition. Only later in the story does work take on a difficult dimension, becoming an element of life that people would sometimes rather avoid. But this is not the end of the story.

With the coming of Christ and the eruption of the Reign or Kingdom of God, the human condition is redeemed, raised up again, restored to its former condition—at least it is beginning to be so. The Kingdom of God is not fully here yet, it is "in-process." Only at the "final coming of Christ"—whatever this metaphorical religious language may mean—will God's Reign be complete.

All the same, even now we begin to benefit from the effects of Christ's coming into the world, the presence of the risen Christ in our midst, and the impact this has on human existence in general. Even though work often retains its "sweat of your brow" character, still, human work is part of God's original plan for human existence and is redeemed in Christ.

Therefore, work is an important part of who we are and of the meaning of life.

Most people experience this positive dimension of work, because most people would rather work than not work. Many times we complain about the need to "go to work," but just take our work away from us and we complain even more. Many people enjoy the work they do, and it's not unusual for people to dread retirement if it means no more work to do. "Retired" people often stay just as involved with work—on a volunteer basis, for example—as people who are not retired. Pope John Paul II said: "Work is not a curse, it is a blessing from God who calls [us] to rule the earth and transform it, so that the divine work of creation may continue with [our] intelligence and effort."

Work is not just something we "do," it is part of who we are and a big part of how most people have an impact on the world. Vanessa, a young woman in her mid-twenties, looks at her work as not just work but a way to express her Catholic faith. "When I graduated from college and went to work I used to think of my job as 'just a job,'" she explained. "But then I got involved in a discussion group for young adults, in my parish, and we read a book about how work is a way to live your faith. Now I see that how I do my work is basic to my Christian identity."

What Vanessa said is true regardless of the kind of work a person does, whether you're a brain surgeon, a worker in a fast food restaurant, a bus driver, farmer, teacher, sales person, retail clerk, lawyer, mechanic, dentist, journalist, computer technician, or whatever. Any kind of work has several aspects, all of which relate to one's faith and spirituality.

Work is a way to make a living. Regardless of the kind of work we do it is a way to earn the money we need to live, to buy the groceries, pay the rent or make the mortgage payments, buy clothing, pay our utility bills, pay for transportation, and so forth. On this level, our main concern is usually the amount of money we earn. We need enough to pay the bills, of course, but on the level of faith the question takes on another perspective.

On the level of faith, the question looks like this: How much is enough? We live in a culture that insists there is no such thing as enough. Unless you are quite wealthy, you don't have enough money, your house isn't good enough, and neither is your furniture. Your car isn't fancy enough, you don't have enough new clothes, and your cat is living a deprived existence. There is no such thing as "enough."

From a Catholic faith perspective most of us arrive at "enough" long before we think we do. From a Catholic faith perspective the purpose of life is not to reach ever higher levels of affluence, the purpose of life is love of God and other people. From a Catholic faith perspective we ask if working sixty, seventy or more hours a week in order to make more and more money is a healthy way to use the limited time we have. Do we live to work or work to live? "Work is for man," says the *Catechism of the Catholic Church,* "not man for work" (no. 2428).

Rick, a Catholic in his late twenties, grinned a bit sheepishly as he talked about how he spent his first few years after college. "I worked my tail off," Rick said, "I burned the midnight oil, burned the candle at both ends, and burned myself out. Totally. I was so convinced that becoming a big success with the company I worked for was the answer to all of life's problems. Then it dawned on me that life is too short to work like that, so many long hours, hardly ever doing anything but working, eating on the run, sleeping, and commuting. It was crazy, absolutely insane."

Rick was fortunate enough to find a job in a midsize city with a smaller company. "The owners are very big on employees living a healthy lifestyle and spending time with their families and so forth," Rick said. "I'm single, but the same values apply to me. They told me that if I couldn't get my work done in a forty-hour work week it would just have to wait until next week. This is a very successful company, too. I think healthy, happy employees make for success in business, as well."

Work is a way to have an impact on society. Regardless of the kind of work we do it has an effect on the big wide world out there. Most kinds of work benefit society, but we must admit that there are some kinds of work society could probably do without. It is even possible that some kinds of work that are considered highly respectable may fall into this category. From a Catholic perspective we need to ask the question about the impact of our work. Does it help people or take advantage of people? Does it benefit society or drag it down?

Almost any kind of work can be done in a way to benefit others or harm them. A teacher who does a poor job of teaching should look for another line of work. A truck driver who regularly backs into buildings and other vehicles should find a job driving a smaller truck. An unscrupulous lawyer or physician is no help to society.

Our work is not merely "helpful" to society, however. It actually has a theological meaning. *"Human work* proceeds directly from persons created in the image of God and called to prolong the work of creation by subduing the earth, both with and for one another . . ." says the *Catechism of the Catholic Church.* "Work honors the Creator's gifts and the talents received from him. It can also be redemptive" (no. 2427).

When we do our work well, when we make it a way to love God and neighbor, when our work makes use of our God-given talents and gifts, it becomes *redemptive,* that is, it brings healing and draws the world closer to its Creator.

Work is a way to love our neighbor. From a Catholic faith perspective whatever work we do we are called by Christ to make it a way to be of service to others and give witness to God's love for the world. We are called to give our employer an honest day's work for an honest wage. We are called to treat our fellow employees and customers or clients with respect. Indeed, our fellow employees and those we work for are the "neighbors" Christ invites us to love as we love ourselves.

Some professions or jobs lend themselves in obvious ways to serving our neighbor. People in the medical professions, teachers, counselors, psychologists, and social workers involve themselves in work designed to help others. Bus drivers, airline pilots, and others in transportation industries help us get where we want to go and back again. Day care providers offer a safe environment for children while parents work, a sacred trust if ever there was one. Nursing home personnel provide a caring environment for elderly people who need help getting along from day to day. Farmers provide food for the rest of us to buy at grocery stores and supermarkets. Clergy and vowed religious clearly dedicate their lives to serving others in numerous ways.

Many other kinds of work may not lend themselves to such an obvious connection with a dedication to loving our neighbor. Sometimes it all depends on the attitude of the worker. A person involved in sales may be motivated by greed or by a genuine desire to serve others and make a living at the same time. The advertising industry can either serve people or take advantage of them. An investment counselor can have his or her own bank account uppermost in mind or the good of the client as the primary concern. It all depends on the motivation and perspective of the worker.

Work is a way to find personal meaning and fulfillment. Most people look for work that they will enjoy, that has meaning for them on a personal level, something they can believe in. If we choose work based entirely on how much money it will enable us to accumulate, that's a good way to become spiritually and emotionally unbalanced—"sick," even. So it's important to choose work that suits our interests, abilities, and talents.

Here is where we make contact most clearly with the divine meaning of work. God calls us to a vocation—to marriage, parent-hood, a single life, or life as a priest or vowed religious—as our basic life orientation, our most basic way to live out our baptismal promises. But by extension, God also calls us to be for others and work out our salvation by having a positive impact on the world in which we live. Through our work we find God and share God's love for the world. It's as simple—and profound—as that.

There was a time when many people found a line of work and stayed with it for thirty or forty years, but that era is gone. There is a good chance that even if you have a profession for which you trained many years you may apply your knowledge and skills in several ways in the course of your lifetime. Most peo-ple change jobs several times over a span of thirty years. This requires a spirituality that is willing to trust that God will lead us into vari-ous kinds of work that suit our abilities and personal qualities.

At one time or another, many people find it necessary to cope with being unemployed involuntarily. Such times may last a few weeks or many months. Being unemployed can be a terribly difficult experience, but like all human experiences it is also one in which we encounter God's love and find opportunities to grow in love and grow deeper in faith.

This does not mean, of course, that being unemployed will ever be fun. Each person will experience unemployment in a unique fashion because each person is unique. Still, there are some common aspects to the experience of being involuntarily unemployed.

Assuming a physical disability does not rule out employment entirely, an important part of being unemployed is obvious—the need to look for employment. In this sense, being unemployed is hard work. Looking for work can be a tedious, sometimes frightening, discouraging project. Not only does it require practical job-hunting skills, but it also requires hope and trust. Looking for work requires us to not give up. It requires prayer. In *The Spirituality of Work: Unemployed Workers* (ACTA Publications, 1993), author Joseph Gossé wrote:

> Unemployment does not lie outside the range of God's power or presence. It can be a fertile field to be harvested, but only by the worker ready to do so. Unemployed workers must maintain an attitude of receptivity to the transcendent. God uses a variety of unexpected tools to break through to us.
>
> These might include a friendly conversation, a sermon, a counseling session, a retraining program, or a job tip or reference.

It might even be necessary for family, friends or colleagues to prod unemployed workers to "get to work." The divine help offered may seem at first to be insignificant, but faith teaches us that something that appears small eventually can make a huge difference in our lives.

Being involuntarily unemployed is one of those times in our life when we find out who we really are. We cope with unemployment as we cope with life. If I were a prayerful person who tried to base my life on my faith before I was unemployed, I would cope with unemployment in a prayerful, faith-based manner. Of course, sometimes finding oneself unemployed can be the kick in the pants we need to turn us back to a more conscious relationship with God. It can spark us to get back to being a more prayerful person than we were before.

No matter what our work may be—even if our work right now is being unemployed and looking for paid employment—we find God and God's will for us in our work. Here is where our work and our spirituality come into communion with each other.

As human beings created in the image of God, healed and raised up by Christ, we live our faith by everything we do, including our work. Some people think that in order to "give witness" to our faith we must verbalize it as often as possible. Catholicism, however, retains the ancient Christian conviction that words can be easy and cheap. Sure, it's good to be able to discuss our faith if the occasion calls for it. But the most important and effective way we witness to our faith is by our actions.

When we do our work in a manner that shows love for God and other people, in a way that reveals an honest spirit and integrity, that says much to the world about our faith.

"In response to the question about the first of the commandments, Jesus says: 'The first is, "Hear, O Israel: The Lord our God, the Lord is one; and you shall love the Lord your God with all your heart, and with all your soul, and with all your mind, and with all your strength." The second is this, "You shall love your neighbor as yourself." There is no other commandment greater than these' [Mark 12:29–31]."

Catechism of the Catholic Church
(no. 2196)

CHAPTER
4

Personal Relationships

What do our personal relationships have to do with being Catholic? Truth to tell, you can't get any closer to the heart of the matter. Luke's version of the Great Commandment of Jesus goes like this: "You shall love the Lord your God with all your heart, and with all your soul, and with all your strength, and with all your mind; and your neighbor as yourself" (10:27).

So basic is this truth that the opening words of the *Catechism of the Catholic Church* focus on it: "God . . . created man to make him share in his own blessed life . . . He calls together all men . . . " (no. 1).

Personal relationships are the essence of being a follower of Christ. There is much we can say about faith that is true, several ways to describe faith. But rock bottom faith is a personal relationship with God, which makes our relationships with other people inseparable from our relationship with our Creator. Karl Rahner, S.J. said: "There is no love for God that is not, in itself, already a love for neighbor; and love for God only comes to its own identity through its fulfillment in a love for neighbor. Only one who loves his or her neighbor can know who God actually is. And only one who ultimately loves God . . . can manage unconditionally to abandon himself or herself to another person . . . "

Pause for a minute and think about the most significant experiences or events in your life. How many of these relate directly to personal relationships? Chances are the events in your life that influenced you the most were closely related to family, friends, and teachers. These are the people who make us who we are, and in the long run these are the people who help us to know God. It is also through our responses to these people, and to God, that we make ourselves who we are.

Saint Thomas Aquinas studied under Saint Albert the Great at the University of Paris, but he made a poor impression on his fellow students. They nicknamed him "the dumb ox." Albert called Thomas to a private interview during which the two men discussed all the subjects in the university curriculum. At his next lecture, Albert told the class, "You call your brother Thomas a dumb ox; let me tell you that one day the whole world will listen to his bellowings." Aquinas went on to become the most important and influential theologian in the history of the church.

Imagine what an impact Albert had on Thomas. Had Albert never talked privately with Thomas it's possible that Thomas might have come to believe his fellow students and become a "dumb ox." Because—in part, at least—his teacher took an interest in him, took the trouble to find out what he was really like, then stood up for him before his peers, Thomas Aquinas became a great teacher himself and a great saint.

How many of us can tell similar stories? For God works through our personal relationships to bring us to birth in the fullest sense of the word. Through our parents, brothers and sisters, friends, teachers, and later through our own family relationships, our work supervisors and fellow employees, God draws us out of ourselves toward our deepest self and toward the mystery of our own divine destiny.

How can this be? The mystery is at once simple and profound. For in other people we encounter the Cross and Resurrection of Christ, a mystery into which we are initiated at Baptism. Even those we love most dearly are frequently difficult to live with, but by doing so—by accepting the "cross" dimension of our relationships with them—we find ourselves being raised up; we become deeper, more caring people, more capable of genuine love for others.

No one grows up in a perfect family. We all have imperfect parents, irritating siblings, and peculiar aunts, uncles, and cousins. In some cases, people grow up in genuinely "dysfunctional" families. Sometimes our families give us as much to overcome as they give us the resources we need to become independent, healthy individuals. What can we say about such situations? We can say this, that even our negative experiences can help us grow up if we allow them to.

Sometimes we overlook the holy when it is right before our eyes, and sometimes we overlook grace—God's self-gift—because it looks as ordinary as an old shoe. Indeed, sometimes the sacred is extremely inconvenient because it is in our everyday, irritating relationships with family and friends. We don't think this is how God should come to us, right here in this spouse, or this child, or this neighbor, or this fellow worker. "How could you, God?" we think to ourselves. But this is the mystery, the mystery all around us, that the infinite God, the God whose love has no limits, chooses to be right before our eyes in the people we live and work with daily.

Grace hardly ever comes in a gleaming silver package with a shining golden bow on top. Everyone is both helped and hindered, enabled and disabled, by his or her family of origin. It's all a mixed-up confusion sometimes. Much depends on how we respond to the negative influences in our past. Either we can spend the rest of our life whining about it, or we can learn and move on. Words quoted in an earlier chapter from Saint Paul are appropriate here, too: "We know that all things work together for good for those who love God . . . " (Romans 8:28).

Popular psychology authors and self-help gurus who charge enormous fees on the speaking circuit grow wealthy encouraging what amounts to a thinly veiled exercise in self-pity. Such gurus generally drip with sincerity, but sincerity guarantees nothing. They promote a self-centered search for one's "inner child" and irrational anger at one's parents, siblings, and teachers. There is some value to what such gurus teach, of course, but it is severely limited. Far more helpful are some words of Jesus: "If any want to become my followers, let them deny themselves and take up their cross and follow me. For those who want to save their life will lose it, and those who lose their life for my sake, and for the sake of the gospel, will save it" (Mark 8:34–35).

Of course, we are not wildly enthusiastic about this whole line of thought. Deny myself? Deny my *self*? Holy Toledo. How un-American can you get? Take up my cross—the things in my life that irritate me the most, or cause me the most suffering—take up my cross willingly, accept it without whining or feeling sorry for myself? Give my life away in service to others, even the people I live and work with? Oh, man! But this, this, is the key to a life worth living. Listen, seeker, hard as this saying may be to accept, this is the key to a life worth living, this is the key to a joy unimaginable. Not to always *succeed* at doing this, of course, but to keep on *trying*.

To one degree or another our family of origin cripples us emotionally, even spiritually. But that is the way of the world; it happens to all of us. Some experience more hurt than others, but it happens to everyone. A major part of growing up, of becoming an adult, is growing to the point where we can see our parents and siblings as, like us, imperfect human beings, people hurt by their own family upbringing who, more than likely, did the best they could. A major part of becoming an adult is growing to the point where we can forgive our parents, our siblings, our teachers, for any harm they may have done us.

Forgiveness, seeker, that is a big part of being a Catholic. Can we forgive our parents and teachers? They were not perfect, they made mistakes, they did it wrong sometimes, maybe they hurt us. But it remains true—and this is sometimes very hard to believe, very difficult to accept—they loved us truly all the same, and they love us today. Can we accept this? Maybe it was in their own difficult-to-understand way, but they loved us all the same, and they wanted the best for us. They had their hurts, too.

We can't go through life blaming our family of origin for our problems. Sooner or later, we need to forgive, put it behind us, take responsibility for ourselves, and get on with it. Otherwise, we are liable to spend the rest of our lives wallowing in self-pity. Sooner or later, we must *choose* to grow up if we expect to have any life at all. Sooner or later, either we choose to put the past behind us, or we choose self-pity as a way of life, which is a pathetic choice.

For most people, the personal relationship that has the most potential to help us grow up, to draw us out of ourselves, and open us to ongoing loving intimacy with God is the permanent, committed relationship called marriage. If you are single, you may or may not have marriage in mind as a possibility, of course. What's important is that you try to be open-minded. Some people plan to marry but never do. Others don't expect to marry but they do all the same. Perhaps the most Catholic of positions is to remain open to surprises, for we have a surprising God.

Whether you marry or not, it's important to have a clear understanding of the Catholic concept of love. We view love in various ways, but when it comes to relationships our tradition is above all realistic and wise. Catholicism insists that the most powerful, most reliable form of love is the kind that does not depend on our emotions. As we noted in an earlier chapter, Saint Thomas Aquinas gave the best-known expression to this understanding when he said that to love is to will the good of the other.

This most reliable kind of love is an act of the will, a choice, that does not rely upon feelings. This is the kind of love that enabled Mother Teresa to see the human dignity of people dying in the gutters of Calcutta and take them to a place where they can at least receive a caring touch and a gentle word before they die. Mother Teresa made the choice to love these people in spite of all appearances. There was nothing romantic about it.

The choice to will the good of the other is the kind of love that enables us to overlook one another's mistakes, irritating habits, even the ways we hurt one another, both intentionally and unintentionally. The choice to will the good of the other is the kind of love that enables a man and woman to remain married to one another "for as long as we both shall live." Remarkably, it is also this kind of love that, over the long haul, enables husband and wife to keep alive the flame of romantic love.

In the dominant North American culture, where the divorce statistics are sky high, this understanding of marriage is clearly counter-cultural. For Catholics, marriage is one of the seven official sacraments of the church. This means that for Catholics, marriage is not just a convenient arrangement but a way to be lovingly intimate with each other in the context of loving intimacy with the risen Christ. Married Catholics go about being Christians precisely by being married.

So fundamental are personal relationships to Catholicism's self-understanding that according to official church teachings, the family — not the parish — is the most basic form of faith community. Ultimately, the quality of life in your local parish depends on the quality of life in the households that constitute the parish. If faith is foundational to the everyday lives of the people who constitute the parish then faith will be vibrant and active in the parish.

Historically, the roots of this insight go back to the earliest days of the Christian community. Since the mid-sixteenth century, however, following the Protestant Reformation and the Council of Trent, which launched the Catholic Counter-Reformation, Catholic leaders cultivated a parish-based understanding of the church. The first thing Catholics thought of when they thought of the church was their parish. If something "religious" happened, it happened in one's parish. Today, more and more parishes encourage a family-centered perspective.

This does not mean that we overlook or discount single and widowed people. Rather, the point is that everyone has family relationships, and those relationships are basic to our experience of Christian faith. The extended family relationships of single and widowed people continue to be basic to their lives, and such people ordinarily have relationships with friends that are important to them. Everyone has family relationships, and those relationships are foundational to one's relationship with God. Therefore, parishes need to nourish family and friendship in as many ways as possible.

All this said, it remains true that in parishes Catholicism's self-understanding is based upon the theological importance of personal relationships. From the Catholic perspective it is not possible to be a Christian in private. Faith is not a "God-and-me" affair, it's a "God-and-us" affair. We go to God together or we don't go at all. In the words of Dorothy Day (1897–1980), co-founder of the Catholic Worker movement and one of the most important American Catholics of the twentieth century: "The only answer in this life, to the loneliness we are all bound to feel, is community. The living together, working together, sharing together, loving God and loving our brother [and sister], and living close to [them] in community so we can show our love for Him."

Sometimes Catholics understand this notion of "community" in superficial ways. For Catholicism at its best, community is more than a kind of convivial, back-slapping, hale-fellow-well-met, coffee-and-donuts-after-Mass groupiness. We live in an era that craves this kind of "togetherness," it's true. Loneliness is rampant, and Twelve-Step recovery programs and therapeutic groups of other kinds are common. Sometimes people choose a church community primarily because they like the "fellowship" they find there; people put much energy into conviviality. But the Catholic vision of community is deeper and broader than this.

The Catholic sense of community is rooted in a traditional insight that views the community of believers as "the Mystical Body of

Christ." Scripturally, this idea comes from Saint Paul. In the Letter to the Romans, for example, Paul declares that "we, who are many, are one body in Christ, and individually we are members one of another" (12:5). And in the First Letter to the Corinthians: "Now you are the body of Christ and individually members of it" (12:27).

The *Catechism of the Catholic Church* puts it this way: "The Church is the Body of Christ. Through the Spirit and his action in the sacraments, above all the Eucharist, Christ, who once was dead and is now risen, establishes the community of believers as his own Body" (no. 805).

While you may find plenty of glad-handing conviviality in some Catholic parishes, in others you will not. In both cases, however, the "sense of community" is just as real if you look below the surface. In a parish where official smiling greeters grab your hand and pump it enthusiastically as you walk in the church on a Sunday morning, you may feel welcome and part of a community as a result. Don't be put off, however, by a parish where there are no smiling "greeters" at the door, where you quietly enter church, find yourself a pew, and wait for the liturgy to begin.

In both situations, the deepest experience of community comes from the conviction that the community is the Mystical Body of Christ. It's a more contemplative experience; one that comes from giving your whole self to participation in the liturgy and to living your faith on a daily basis. Conviviality can be a superficial experience unless it is rooted in this deeper experience of the Body of Christ.

Being Catholic means that we find in personal relationships a deeper, sacred dimension. In our marriages, families, friendships, and parish community we find not mere accidental interactions with other people who are incidental to who we are and what life is about. Rather, in all of these personal relationships we find God and the love of God. It's a tremendous mystery and a holy one. In our personal relationship with God we find ourselves moved to care for and serve other people; and in our personal relationships with people we find ourselves attracted to the love of God. It's a profound mystery, and a holy one.

"The Lord leads all persons by paths and in ways pleasing to him, and each believer responds according to his heart's resolve and the personal expressions of his prayer."

Catechism of the Catholic Church
(no. 2699)

Personal Prayer and Spirituality

Faith, at its most basic, is a personal relationship with God. Seeker, take note. We do not need to go in search of God for we already *have* God, or rather, God has us. Faith is a human experience, an experience of loving intimacy with, to repeat Dante's words, "the Love that moves the sun and the other stars."

Faith is a personal relationship but not in exactly the same way as two people have a relationship. Again, we're up to our eyes in metaphors and analogies. Our relationship with God is different because we are not here and God is not over there. Rather, as Saint

Augustine said more than fifteen hundred years ago, God is closer to us than we are to ourselves. Our personal relationship with God is an accomplished fact, and with God's help we can cultivate an awareness of this. God lives in us, and we live in God. There is no separating ourselves from God's loving presence.

The most important form of Catholic prayer is the Eucharist or Mass. The Eucharist is the "source and summit" of our life as a faith community. But because faith is an everyday and everywhere reality, this means that prayer is an everyday and everywhere activity. Being a prayerful person distinguishes those whose Catholic faith is central to their existence from those for whom their relationship with God is peripheral. Those who sense God's constant loving presence can't help but be prayerful people.

Prayer, from a Catholic perspective, is not a matter of addressing a God who is distant but a God who dwells in us. For Catholicism, prayer is more *communion* than communication. Prayer is not a matter of chasing after a retreating God, or pleading with God to pay attention to us, or begging God to take care of us—although sometimes we naturally do this. Our God does not play "hide 'n seek" with us. Rather, for Catholics prayer is more a matter of *reminding ourselves* about God's unconditional love for us, renewing our awareness of God's constant love, a love that is absolutely trustworthy. Prayer involves giving ourselves to this love.

Sometimes people confuse "saying prayers" with prayer. To recite a prayer does not automatically mean we are praying. Sure, sometimes we pray by reading prayers from a book, which is perfectly fine. Some of the greatest saints insisted that such prayer is best on a day-in, day-out basis. Sometimes we pray by reciting memorized traditional prayers such as the Our Father, the Hail Mary, and so forth. Sometimes we can pray no other way. But the essence of prayer, from a Catholic perspective, is something simpler and deeper, something interior. Even when we recite formal prayers, the ideal is for such prayers to express this deeper prayer. Prayer at its most basic is a *simple conscious awareness of God's loving presence in and around me at all times.* Thomas Merton said it as well as anyone ever has. He said: "How I pray is breathe."

Personal prayer relies on what might be called a spirit of loving devotion to God. Love of God and neighbor are foundational to any Christian life, and Catholicism takes both to heart. If we are open to God's love for us we will become aware of how overwhelming that love is, and when we become aware of that we will be moved to respond with a spirit of loving devotion to God. We will respond to God's love with love in return. Sometimes prayer is like this, being still in God's loving presence and responding with love in return.

In an article, "The Eclipse of Love for God," published in the Jesuit weekly magazine, *America* (9 March 1996), Father Edward Collins Vacek, S.J., discusses the importance of loving God directly in addition to active love for other people. "Just as we must eat and think and play, or else we wither and die," Father Vacek wrote, "and just as we must develop good relations with other human beings if we are to develop as persons, so also we cannot hope to become fully human unless we love God."

Because we are essentially relational beings, Father Vacek continues, we become stunted when our relational capacities go unattended. We have an in-born desire and capacity for God, and our deepest self will dry up unless we nourish it by loving God directly. "Hence, in order to become fully who we are, we must be growing in love for God."

People who love God engage in activities you won't find in the lives of other people. We engage in tried-and-true ways to cultivate a loving relationship with God. We attend Mass regularly, make retreats, and try to be generally prayerful persons. We try to be open to God's guidance and grace in our daily lives. We read and pray with the Scriptures and pay particular attention to the person of Jesus and his words and example in the Gospels. "Those who are not in a personal relationship with the Christian God," Father Vacek explains, "will not do these sorts of things, and so they cannot similarly develop this most important dimension of human life."

All well and good. But as seekers, what if we find this line of thought puzzling? Actually, it's nothing to be concerned about. Being Catholic is a lifelong learning process, and the important thing is to remain open and willing to grow . . . for a lifetime. The first step in loving God directly is not to strain and sweat trying to "love God." Rather, the first step is to be open and receptive to God's love for you. In quiet moments simply open your heart to God's love for you, allow this absolute, unconditional love to touch and move you. From time to time, you may repeat a silent prayer, something like this: "Help me to know your love, O God." Soon you will feel moved to return God's love for you with love for God in return.

There is a strand of Catholic spirituality that lends itself particularly well to being open to God's love and loving God in return. It's called "devotionalism." Thus, there are many

traditional Catholic "devotions," forms of
prayer directed to loving God. Sometimes
devotions focus on the Eucharist, the Blessed
Virgin Mary, or one of the saints, which are
also ways to love God.

Devotions—which we will discuss in more
detail in Chapter 7—are personal forms of
prayer, and they can take many shapes. A
devotion is simply a way to spend a few
moments opening your heart to God. You may
find traditional prayers helpful, or you may
find that the church's Liturgy of the Hours, or
some modification of it, suits you best. This latter devotion has the advantage of keeping you
in touch with Scripture. The Liturgy of the
Hours gives you Psalms, other readings from
the Bible, and short prayers from other
sources, all organized to be prayed at various
times throughout the day, especially morning
and evening.

Having said all this, however, make no mistake about it: Most Catholics do not become
highly organized about their prayers, devotions, and so forth. Brother Lawrence of the
Resurrection, a seventeenth-century French
monk, is the author of a spiritual classic called
The Practice of the Presence of God. In this wonderful little book, Brother Lawrence emphasizes
God's presence in every moment of the day. "It
is not needful always to be in church to be with

God," he said. "We can make a chapel of our heart, to which we can from time to time withdraw to have gentle, humble, loving communion with him. Everyone is able to have these familiar conversations with God, some more, some less—he knows our capabilities. Let us make a start."

Brother Lawrence's words carry a core insight that is essential to the place of prayer in any Catholic life. Prayer is not, first of all, an esoteric activity we engage in only at special times and places under formal circumstances. Rather, for Catholicism prayer is a daily and ordinary activity appropriate to any time and place. In the Gospels, Jesus tells us that God is our *Abba,* an Aramaic word almost always translated "Father," which means something more like "loving Papa." We live and breathe the mystery of a constant loving intimacy with our God, therefore prayer—conscious, perhaps inarticulate, communion with God—is appropriate no matter where we are or what we are doing.

Of course, we can't be consciously praying all the time. But as Brother Lawrence taught, we can and should turn to God in our heart at any time while working or walking, waiting or playing, relaxing or taking a bath.

One of the reasons Catholicism cherishes the arts is because they help us to be mindful

of God's constant loving presence. On an
everyday popular level, Catholics often keep
"sacred art" around for precisely this reason.
Something as simple as a traditional or more
contemporary "holy card," stuck on a nearby
bulletin board or refrigerator door, is a
reminder of the holy present in the ordinary.
Such a thing can be a gentle reminder to turn
our heart to God.

One of the most popular forms of Catholic
devotional prayer is the Rosary. For many centuries, through constant social and cultural
change, Catholics have retained a special affec-
tion for the Rosary. Something about the repet-
itive nature of the prayers, and the simplicity of
the mysteries that go with each set of ten Hail
Marys, touches the Catholic heart. The Rosary
is a physical form of prayer, and being embod-
ied spirits we appreciate a form of prayer that
gives us something to hang onto. The beads of
a rosary slip through our fingers as we pray,
and that can be a comfort.

There are many pious little books and
leaflets about the Rosary that are probably
harmless and may be helpful. Such resources
may perpetuate the misconception, however,
that the Rosary is a rather childish form of
prayer. The educated reader who wants to gain
a more in-depth understanding of the Rosary
would do well to consult one of the more artic-

ulate recent works published on the subject. In his excellent book, *A Western Way of Meditation: The Rosary Revisited* (Loyola Press, 1991), David Burton Bryan, Ph.D., says that the Rosary is "clearly the world's single most popular form of meditation."

Perhaps the most truthful statement anyone can make about prayer is to say that prayer is a mystery. Prayer is a mystery because in prayer we acknowledge that there is an emptiness in our deepest center that only God can fill. You are a finite, limited being, yet in your deepest center there is a pocket, a void, a "space," that only the infinite God can fill. Each one of us has a hunger and a thirst that only God can satisfy. Often people try to fill this divine emptiness by becoming workaholics, or they try to satisfy their hunger for God with everything from sex, drugs, and/or alcohol, to nicotine, food, and/or a packed social calendar. Once again, Saint Augustine hit the nail on the head when he said in his *Confessions* that "our hearts are restless until they rest in Thee." Thomas Merton, in *No Man Is an Island*, wrote:

> Prayer is inspired by God in the depth of our own nothingness. It is the movement of trust, or gratitude, of adoration, or of sorrow that places us before God, seeing

both Him and ourselves in the light of His infinite truth, and moves us to ask Him for the mercy, the spiritual strength, the material help that we all need. The man whose prayer is so pure that he never asks God for anything does not know who God is, and does not know who he is himself: for he does not know his own need of God.

Granted that prayer is fundamental to an everyday life of faith, still it is not "the whole enchilada." Prayer is *part* —an essential part, but still only a part —of a mature Catholic spirituality. "Spirituality" is one of those traditional religious words we may easily misunderstand. This term should not suggest activities that have little or nothing to do with "the real world" where we live our lives. We are spiritual beings, body and soul, and the world is a spiritual place, visible and invisible. So when we talk about spirituality we talk about cultivating and living what is deepest and most important to us right here, right now.

Indeed, a Catholic spirituality grounds us in the present moment. The past is gone, the future is not here. All we have is the present. The present moment is all we ever have to work with, and we are free to do with it what we choose. Catholic spirituality encourages us to center ourselves in the present moment, accept it as a priceless gift from God, and do something good with it.

For Catholics, our spirituality is difficult to separate from our lifestyle. How we live, the work we do, the ways we use our time and spend our money, our relationships with other people and with the earth, our ideals and goals, what we love and what we despise, all these have a place in our spirituality. From a Catholic perspective, "spirituality" refers to life under the influence of the risen Christ, life open to the guidance of the Holy Spirit, life nourished by an ongoing communion with the love of God.

"Spirituality" refers to the ways we try to cultivate love for God and neighbor, but it also refers to our experience of that love. At the same time a Catholic spirituality is influenced by Sacred Tradition—God's presence in our midst and in the church's people, institutions, and leaders—and by centuries-old customs and traditions.

Perhaps the most basic "spiritual" line of questioning anyone can face would go something like this: Who or what calls the shots in my life? Are the values that shape my heart and my life rooted in my Catholic faith, or do they come from someplace else—the dominant popular culture, for example? Do my actions and choices reflect the values and attitudes of the entertainment and advertising industries, or do they reflect the values and goals I find in the life, death, and Resurrection of Jesus the Christ and in the deepest and best Catholic perspectives on significant life issues? Sometimes these two sources overlap, of course; it's not as if the entertainment and advertising industries are in every respect, at all times, in conflict with Catholic values and perspectives. This happens often enough, however, to make this line of questioning perfectly valid.

One of the best exercises anyone can engage in is to ask this question: What do I think is the purpose of life? Of course, we are likely to kid ourselves when we respond to this question. One way to find out what you really think is the purpose of life is to look squarely at how you spend your time and how you spend your money. Get out your calendar and your bank statement. Look over how you spent your time and money for the last six months.

Being Catholic means believing—and acting as if—the purpose of life is to love God and neighbor. Being Catholic means we spend our time and money in ways that serve this purpose. A person who gives only lip service to this ideal will spend his or her time and money in ways that are fundamentally self-centered. It's as simple as that. Sometimes, of course, such a line of self-questioning can be discouraging. Few of us live our faith as deeply or well as we might. The important thing is to be honest about where your heart is. Regardless of how well you live up to what you say you believe, what do you care about most deeply? If love of God and loving service to others fits into your response, you're doing fine.

This does not mean that we must spend most of our time working in some heroic charitable activity. It's a question of focus. What are your most basic motives for doing what you do? Say you attend college or work. Why are you in college? Is your dominant motive to gain knowledge and skills that will enable you to become wealthy? Fine. The question is, what do you plan to do with your wealth once you gain it? Do you plan to hoard it, or do you plan to share it? Do you plan to become as comfortable and secure as possible, and the rest of the world can take care of itself? Or do you plan to use your wealth, at least in part, to help those less fortunate than yourself?

Perhaps your motive for attending college is more directly altruistic. You want to enter a profession geared to helping people in some way or gain skills that clearly have some social value. Perhaps you plan to become a teacher, enter a medical profession, or start a service-oriented business of some kind. In such circumstances we again are faced with the question of motive, for even such apparently altruistic plans can still be self- rather than other-centered. Of course, it's the rare person whose motives are one hundred percent unselfish. Still, this is a line of self-examination that we never outgrow.

The main point of all this is quite simple, really. Our spirituality cannot be separated from our life as a whole. Life and spirituality are one. For Catholics, our spirituality is how we live our life in ongoing loving intimacy with God present in ourselves, in our world, and in all the ways we use the limited time we have upon the earth. Being Catholic includes being a prayerful person and being a person whose fundamental goals focus on love of God and neighbor. This is what spirituality and prayer are all about.

"Participation in the communal celebration of the Sunday Eucharist is a testimony of belonging and of being faithful to Christ and to his Church. The faithful give witness by this to their communion of faith and charity. Together they testify to God's holiness and their hope of salvation. They strengthen one another under the guidance of the Holy Spirit."

Catechism of the Catholic Church
(no. 2182)

Sacraments, Liturgies, and Parishes

If there is anything that distinguishes Catholicism from Protestant expressions of Christianity it is Catholic sacramentalism. Catholics find hints of God and rumors of angels, reflections of the Divine Mystery and echos of heaven almost everyplace they look. God is just around every corner and barely hidden under every leaf. For classical Protestantism—not to say all modern forms of Protestantism—the world and human nature are radically "fallen," almost completely corrupt, and God is like a gigantic spiritual helicopter that swoops down and rescues us from all this evil and rottenness.

Catholicism takes human sinfulness seriously, of course, but it also takes quite seriously and with joy the words of Saint Paul: "Ever since the creation of the world [God's] eternal power and divine nature, invisible though they are, have been understood and seen through the things he has made" (Romans 1:20).

Being Catholic includes the understanding that because the Son of God became human, all that is human has been transformed. All that is human mirrors that which is divine. A baby's smile or the shocking sartorial habits of a teenager, both can tell us something about God. We can find echos of the gospel in a newspaper comic strip or popular music. A mother's love and a father's love can both give hints of what God's love is like. Both the powerful, spectacular roar of Niagra Falls and a silent sunset can manifest God's presence.

In her novel *Little Altars Everywhere* (Broken Moon Press, 1992/HarperCollins, 1996), author Rebecca Wells illustrates the Catholic sacramental worldview. Wells' character Siddalee Walker, about age nine, describes a dream she has sometimes. She swings in her backyard at her home near Thornton, Louisiana:

> We are swinging high, flying way up, higher than in real life. And when I look down, I see all the ordinary stuff—our

brick house, the porch, the tool shed, the back windows, the oil-drum barbecue pit, the clothesline, the china-berry tree. But they are all lit up from inside so their every-day selves have holy sparks in them, and if people could only see those sparks, they'd go and kneel in front of them and pray and just feel good. Somehow the whole world looks like little altars everywhere. And everytime [we] fly up into the air and then dive down to earth, it's like we're bowing our heads at those altars and we are pray-ing and playing all at the same time.

Catholicism believes that God is at home in the world, that "the whole world looks like lit-tle altars everywhere." Being Catholic means cultivating the perception that God is every-place, therefore God is in particular places, too. Because God is both everyplace and right here in this place, Catholics are not surprised to learn that the risen Christ chose to give himself to his people in seven special ways. These are, of course, the seven official sacraments of the church: Baptism, Confirmation, Eucharist, Reconciliation, Marriage, Holy Orders, and Anointing of the Sick.

In each of these rites and rituals Christ shares himself in a particular way with those open to his presence. To be an adult Catholic is to recognize and welcome these sacraments into your life. They are a manifestation of Christ's desire to touch your life with his love in ways you can touch, taste, smell, hear, and see.

Many people willingly grant that God is everywhere, but they find it difficult to believe that God can be anyplace in particular—in bread and wine, for example, or in the pouring of water over an infant's forehead, or in the love of a married couple, or in words of forgiveness and reconciliation spoken by a priest. Catholics welcome the real presence of the Son of God in the community gathered to celebrate Mass; we recognize his presence in the priest who presides at Mass; and we find the risen Christ truly present—his whole person, "body and blood, soul and divinity"—in the consecrated bread and wine. What do we mean by "risen"? It's a mind-boggling mystery, we can grasp with our heart but not with our intellect; a deep and joyful mystery, that is, a deep and joyful manifestation of Christ present in our midst.

In each of the seven sacraments we experience God's love in the risen Christ. In Baptism we become a member of Christ's body, his people, the church. We accept his gift of spiritual healing and liberation ("salvation"), and we commit ourselves to a life united with him and with his people, the church.

In the sacrament of Confirmation we are "more perfectly bound to the church and are enriched with a special strength of the Holy Spirit" (*Catechism of the Catholic Church*, no. 1285). In past decades Confirmation was typically celebrated about the age of twelve or thirteen. Now the trend is to celebrate this sacrament at the same time as First Communion or sometimes later, during the late teens or early twenties. Most likely the normal time for Confirmation will be with First Communion.

Sometimes people have a difficult time understanding the sacrament of Reconciliation — Penance, Confession, Forgiveness, or Conversion, the *Catechism of the Catholic Church* uses all five designations (see nos. 1423–24) — because they wonder why anyone should tell another human being about one's sins or offenses against God. That's just the point, however. Catholicism, you see, is convinced that our sins affect our relationships with other people as much as they affect our relationship with God. This Rite of Forgiveness allows the experience to have both a vertical dimension — God and me — and a horizontal dimension — the church/faith community and me. Human personalities and interaction take on special significance in this sacrament, however, so finding a priest you are comfortable with is particularly helpful.

Certainly God forgives sins the moment we ask forgiveness. But it does us good to bring our sins into the human circle, as well, because they have an impact there. When we confess our sins or sinfulness to a priest we allow God's loving forgiveness to take on flesh; we *hear* the words of forgiveness that touch our hearts in a way keeping it "just between God and me" does not. In the sacrament of Reconciliation a kind of healing and renewal happens that you will find no place else in the world, not on any psychiatrist's couch or in any counselor's office.

In the sacrament of Marriage, husband and wife find the risen Christ present in their love for each other. Their love itself becomes the "outward sign" of God's love for them and for the world. Some theologians suggest that when husband and wife make love they celebrate the sacrament of Marriage in a way similar to the way we celebrate the Eucharist over and over again. Frequent sexual expression of love in marriage is as important to the holiness of marriage as frequent celebration of the Eucharist is to the Christian life in general.

Husband and wife, by their faithful and unconditional love for each other, reflect God's faithful and unconditional love for all people and for all of creation. Thus, marriage is a source of grace—God's self-gift—not only for the married couple but for the church as a whole and for the world at large. Indeed, so unique is the sacrament of Marriage that the priest is not the minister of this sacrament. Rather, the woman and man who marry are the ministers of the sacrament to each other. At a wedding the priest or deacon acts simply as the official witness for the church.

The sacrament of Holy Orders is, of course, the sacrament that makes a baptized man an ordained priest. (Current official church teaching insists that the church has no power to ordain women to the priesthood.) "This sacrament configures the recipient to Christ," says the *Catechism of the Catholic Church,* "by a special grace of the Holy Spirit, so that he may serve as Christ's instrument for his Church" (no. 1581).

Since the earliest days of the Christian community men designated for leadership — liturgical, sacramental, educational, and social — guide the local faith community. This is necessary for both theological and practical reasons. On a practical level, the community needs someone to act as spiritual guide to help it remain faithful to the gospel. On a theological level, the priest becomes one through whom, in a special way, Christ acts and brings about spiritual healing and liberation ("salvation"). As a sacramental minister, the personal weaknesses and foibles of the priest are irrelevant, for Christ acts through him regardless.

The priest has a necessary role in all the sacraments except Marriage. (In an emergency, however it's also possible for anyone, even an unbaptized person, to baptize someone. See *Catechism of the Catholic Church,* no. 1256.) The priest's most prominent role, however, is liturgical when he presides at the celebration of the Eucharist or Mass.

It is important to understand that the priest is not the only one who celebrates the Eucharist. Rather, the community together celebrates. In a very real sense the priest cannot "say Mass" apart from the community of faith. Even on the rare occasion when a priest might say Mass alone, he does so in the spiritual context of the worldwide faith community. "It is the whole *community,* the Body of Christ united with its Head, that celebrates," says the *Catechism of the Catholic Church.* "Liturgical services are not private functions but are celebrations of the Church . . . " (no. 1140).

The word "liturgy" comes from a Greek term, *leitourgia,* which means "public service" or "work" of the people gathered together. We do not attend Mass as spectators; rather, everyone present actively celebrates the liturgy. The priest presides, and only he has the authority and power to speak the words of consecration, but he receives that power and authority from the risen Christ who is active and present *in us, in the community of faith gathered together for Mass.* This is an important part of what it means to say that we all share in the priesthood of Christ (see *Catechism of the Catholic Church,* no. 1591).

Regular participation in the eucharistic liturgy is essential to a life of faith. Earlier generations of Catholics believed that a willful choice to not attend Mass on a given Sunday was a very serious, or "mortal" sin, and current church teachings retain the idea that we have an "obligation" to attend Mass on Sundays if at all possible. Thus, sometimes older Catholics attend Mass each Sunday out of a sense of obligation, but more than that, to avoid sin. This is better than not attending Mass at all, but it certainly is not the ideal motivation. As long as we attend Mass merely because we don't want to "commit a sin," we miss out on the heart of the matter. Ideally, we participate in the Eucharist because we crave it, we want to be there, and we know that we need to be there.

This leads to an important question: Why attend Mass every Sunday or Saturday evening, at the least? If you look back in history you find that Christians began gathering to celebrate the Eucharist on Sundays because Sunday was the day on which the Resurrection of Jesus took place. Gathering for the Eucharist on Sunday became a time to nourish one's faith — one's loving intimacy with the risen Christ — and a time to find support and encouragement from the church or faith community where the risen Christ is present and active. When our relationship with Christ is a daily reality then we want to be with our faith community to celebrate the Eucharist at least on Sundays or Saturday evenings.

Things being what they are, of course, sometimes we find that the liturgy in a particular parish is dull. Sometimes homilies can put you to sleep. Sometimes, though, young adults experience dynamic, meaningful liturgies while in college, at a Newman Center or Catholic college. Then after they graduate they find themselves in an ordinary parish, and the liturgies come as a shock. Ho-hum, back to the real world . . .

What can you do? First, try to understand that given the historical era we live in, this is the way things are. Parishes everywhere struggle with liturgical issues. Find the most satisfying liturgical situation you can, understand that you will never find a perfect liturgy, then get involved in your parish. If you're single, find ways to participate in the life of your parish that make use of your special gifts. Maybe you can help out with youth activities, or maybe you feel attracted to help organize a singles ministry group. Maybe you have a unique idea of your own about how you can do something extra to participate in the life of your parish. Single or married, don't wait around for someone else to ask you to do something. Step forward and get involved.

At all costs, avoid singles groups or activities for couples that have nothing but a social purpose. No such group will survive unless it has a purpose outside itself, some particular service this group can provide to the parish or to the wider community. Dedication to some form of shared service is the only "glue" that will hold a group together. Such a group may meet once each month at a local soup kitchen, help out at a Saint Vincent dePaul facility, or raise funds for parish youth activities. The possibilities are nearly endless.

Parishes are peculiar places, especially for young adults, single or married without children. It's easy to feel "out of it." So many parish activities seem geared to families, children, and older people. Any truth there may be to this should be tempered by the insight that "the squeaky wheel gets the grease." If young adults care enough about involvement in their parish they will "rock the boat" to get some attention. If not much goes on in a particular parish that is attractive to young adults, perhaps it's because not enough young adults make themselves known.

A great parish idea for a young adults group would be to organize an outreach activity to get more people of that age group involved in the life of the parish. Make phone calls, knock on doors, extend invitations, put ads in the newspaper. Be creative about it. Ask young adults to provide input so the parish can be more "young adult friendly." Organize a weekend retreat for single young adults only or for young married couples only.

The *Catechism of the Catholic Church* quotes Saint John Chrysostom, one of the early fathers of the church (late fourth century): "You cannot pray at home as at church, where there is a great multitude, where exclamations are cried out to God as from one great heart, and where there is something more: the union of minds, the accord of souls, the bond of charity, the prayers of the priests" (no. 2226).

These words from the early days of the Christian community have the ring of truth. Peter Burger, a Lutheran sociologist, once wrote that we need a faith community because faith makes of us "cognitive deviants." That is, to embrace the vision and worldview of the gospel is to adopt a perspective that sometimes runs counter to that of the dominant popular culture. If we are to remain faithful to this vision, and live it from our heart on a daily basis, we need a parish community to support, nourish, and encourage us in our faith. We need the help of others if we are to remain Catholic "cognitive deviants," people who think with Christ, live with Christ, and work with Christ.

This is the ultimate purpose of a parish. If we take our faith to heart, we find that we must have a parish community, and we will do whatever is necessary in order to find a parish where we can belong. We will do whatever we must in order to have a place to experience the sacraments, participate in liturgies, and find a sense of community. No matter how much trouble it takes, it's worth the effort.

"The Tradition of the Church proposes to the faithful certain rhythms of praying intended to nourish continual prayer. Some are daily, such as morning and evening prayer, grace before and after meals, the Liturgy of the Hours. Sundays, centered on the Eucharist, are kept holy primarily by prayer."

Catechism of the Catholic Church
(no. 2698)

CHAPTER
7

Devotional Spirituality

"'**Y**ou shall love the Lord your God with all your heart, and with all your soul, and with all your mind.' This is the greatest and first commandment. And a second is like it: 'You shall love your neighbor as yourself'" (Matthew 22:37–39).

If we wish to articulate the response Jesus invites to his presence and to his message, these words from Matthew's Gospel serve in an excellent fashion. We are called, in all that we do and in every aspect of our lives, to show active love for God and other people, particularly those with whom we live and work most closely; that's why Jesus instructs us to love our "neighbor." Scripture scholars and theologians tell us that these two commandments are, in fact, one, or, at the very least, the two cannot be separated. The Greek word translated as "like" in the third sentence of this quotation from Matthew's Gospel, means "the same as," not "similar to." So the commandment to love our neighbor as ourself is "the same as" the commandment to love God.

If priority must be placed on one of the two loves, it would be love of neighbor. Many of the greatest saints and mystics taught that if your neighbor is in need while you are trying to pray you should abandon your prayers in order to care for your neighbor. All the same, as we discussed in Chapter 5, direct love for God is an indispensable part of any Christian life. It is necessary to cultivate a human love for God if we are to be whole, healthy human beings, if we want to be capable of loving our neighbor in a truly unselfish manner.

Father Edward Collins Vacek, S.J., concludes the article quoted in Chapter 5 by insisting that "although love for neighbor and love for self are essential to the Christian life . . . we must not let these wholesome Christian loves eclipse our love for God. That love should be the sun of our lives."

Traditionally, the strand of Catholic spirituality that best facilitates a direct love for God may be called "devotionalism." Devotions are various kinds of prayer and quasi-liturgical activity that express and nourish love for God.

Devotions may be communal or private. Either way, however, you may get the impression that devotions are best left to "simple believers" or the unsophisticated, people with no depth to their theological understanding of faith and the Christian life. Be cautious about such an impression because it can easily lead to a kind of spiritual snootiness or elitism.

Faith is a gift, and faith at its most fundamental is a personal relationship with God. In this sense, faith is the same for everyone, from the most highly educated theologian to the most ordinary, unsophisticated believer. Faith does not come in sizes and shapes; no one's faith is better than someone else's faith. We are all on the same level when it comes to our relationship with God. Although some people are more willing than others to let faith govern their life, we all believe in and have a personal relationship with the same God. Faith is faith is faith.

How we express our faith is a different matter, of course. Those who are more highly educated, in a formal sense, will probably express and nourish their faith in ways that differ from the "simple believer." A person with a Ph.D. in theology will, presumably, have a better understanding of the meaning and purpose of faith. But we shouldn't get carried away here. There is no room for anyone to have an inflated sense of self simply because he or she

has an advanced academic degree in theology.
For even the most highly developed theological
formulations fall short of the Divine Mystery
they attempt to talk about. When push comes
to shove, the human intellect is unable to grasp
God. Ultimately, everyone is on the same level
when it comes to faith.

Everyone is called to love God, therefore
everyone needs a devotional component to his
or her spirituality. What this looks like will
vary from person to person, but we all have
this need. A person who is too sophisticated or
too highly educated to practice devotional
prayer no longer lives his or her faith in its fullness. Such a person risks his or her faith
becoming little more than a "head trip." Devotions—religious observances and forms of
prayer—are essential to any life of faith.

Catholic devotions are distinguished by their
relation to the Eucharist. As we noted earlier,
the Mass is the "summit and source" of Catholic
life. By extension, in order for devotions to fit
into a life of Catholic faith in a balanced manner they need to draw upon and lead back to
the Eucharist. For this reason, although there
are many kinds of devotions, eucharistic devotions take pride of place. Benediction of the
Blessed Sacrament and Adoration of the
Blessed Sacrament, in particular, fit into the
devotional component of Catholic spirituality

because they focus on the consecrated bread, or host, which is set aside after Mass and kept in a tabernacle in a church.

Historically, the early Christians began saving consecrated bread—now no longer mere bread except in appearance—after the eucharistic celebration was over so it could be taken to the sick and those imprisoned for their faith. It is perfectly understandable that Christians would later develop an abiding respect for and devotion to the risen Christ truly and fully present in the consecrated bread.

The main purpose for the consecrated bread and wine is to eat and drink in the course of the liturgy itself, of course. But eucharistic devotions are a natural and legitimate extension of the community's faith in Christ present in its midst. The important thing is for such devotions to nourish faith in the Christ who is present in the community and, especially, who is present in the eucharistic assembly.

Following the Second Vatican Council in the mid-1960s, many Catholic devotions, including eucharistic devotions, fell out of favor in most parishes. This was to be expected during a time when the church tried to refocus its attention on the centrality of the Mass itself, on the essential place of the Scriptures, and on the absolutely basic place of Jesus the risen Christ as the center of our faith. Some three decades later, a swing began to develop back to a more centrist, balanced perspective on the value of devotions—both communal and private—in Catholic life. More and more parishes now schedule Benediction and Adoration of the Blessed Sacrament in ways that maintain the focus on the Liturgy of the Eucharist, or Mass, itself.

Eucharistic adoration has special value not only because it helps us to reflect on the meaning of the Eucharist, but because it helps many people, who might not do so otherwise, to cultivate a contemplative dimension to their spirituality. Some parishes maintain a special place for eucharistic adoration twenty-four hours a day, 365 days a year. This is called "Perpetual Adoration." People sign up in advance to spend an hour or half-hour each week, or once a month, in the presence of the Blessed Sacrament, usually displayed in a special, often gold-plated, sunburst ornament called a "monstrance." For those who participate in eucharistic adoration regularly, this can become a quiet, prayerful, contemplative, very special time, indeed.

In the biweekly Catholic magazine *Commonweal* (19 April 1996), Ann O'Brien Treacy wrote of her monthly experience of eucharistic adoration:

> Whenever I'm asked about the hour vigil I keep, my answer is the same: It's

worth it. I believe you are what you pay attention to . . .

The benefits have spilled over into the other days of my week. I find myself praying more at home. The advantages of giving time to prayer are as tangible as making time to exercise. When I pray regularly I feel spiritually fit like the physical well-being I derive from routine walking or jogging . . . I never find myself tired those days that I get up at 4:14 A.M., and I've been drawn to return many times in addition to "my" hour.

You don't need to be signed up in order to pray at a chapel of perpetual adoration. Just go.

Sometimes parishes or other groups who embrace eucharistic adoration do so for a particular purpose. The purpose may be to pray for respect for life, for an end to world hunger, for the church in general, for the poor, for those with terminal illnesses, for the parish, for healthy marriages, for parents, or for some other intention. In order to maintain a healthy perspective it can be helpful if the sponsoring group provides prayer cards, meditation booklets, and so on, that reflect the vital connections between Adoration of the Blessed Sacrament, the Mass, the parish community, the universal church, and the particular intention for which people are asked to pray.

Eucharistic adoration isn't the only kind of Catholic devotional prayer, of course. Probably the next most popular form of devotion is devotion to Mary, the mother of Jesus. We already discussed the Rosary in some detail in Chapter 5, so there is no need to return to that. The Rosary is, without question, the most popular form of Marian devotion in Christian history, and with good reason. It's a form of prayer that is both easy to follow, easy to practice, and far more contemplative in nature than we sometimes give it credit for. Many Catholics who decided in the years following the Second Vatican Council that they were too sophisticated to pray the Rosary, later searched out their old rosary beads and returned to this quiet, practical form of prayer.

Of course, devotion to Mary takes many forms, sometimes private, sometimes communal. Often, a specific devotion is based on a verified "apparition," or appearance, of Mary. Devotion to Our Lady of Guadalupe, based on a sixteenth-century Marian apparition near present-day Mexico City, has been popular for many centuries among Hispanic Catholics. Mary's appearances to a French peasant girl, Bernadette Soubirous, in the late-nineteenth century, led to devotion to Our Lady of Lourdes. Many thousands of pilgrims visit the shrine at Lourdes every year, some reporting miraculous cures.

Devotion to Mary is not a form of worship. God alone deserves our worship. Sometimes non-Catholics accuse Catholics of Mariolotry, or worship of Mary, but nothing could be further from the truth. Theologically, we pray to Mary as we pray to any of the saints. Although we ask Mary to pray with and for us, we don't believe she has some power independent of the power of God. Fundamentally, Mary is one of us and one of the saints, and we cherish her prayers. Of course, Mary is also the mother of Jesus, the Son of God, so she has a special dignity none of the other saints can claim.

The Second Vatican Council drew on Scripture and ancient Christian tradition and teachings when it taught that Mary is the mother of Jesus, and because the church — meaning all of us — is the body of Christ, she is our mother, too. Mary serves as a model for all believers in her complete gift of herself to the will of God. In the Gospel of Luke, when the angel informs Mary that she is to be the mother of the Messiah, she could have said, "In your dreams, fella." Instead, she replies: "Here am I, the servant of the Lord; let it be with me according to your word" (1:38). This is how we are called to respond to God, as well.

Devotion to the saints is another characteristic of Catholicism. Although it is definitely not required for salvation (spiritual healing and liberation), devotion to the saints has been a part of Christian life since the days of the earliest believers. When they gathered to celebrate the Eucharist the early Christians believed themselves to be in the company of their fellow believers who had died, sometimes as martyrs for the faith. They called on those who had gone ahead of them into eternity to pray for them and to join the earthly community of faith in praying to God.

Later, Christians naturally extended this devotion to saints who had simply lived an exemplary life but had not died for their faith. Saint Martin of Tours (316?–397) seems to have been the first non-martyr to attract such devotion. He was a conscientious objector who wanted to be a monk and reluctantly became a bishop. Martin opposed paganism but pleaded for mercy for heretics, and by his life he mirrored Christ to those who knew him. After his death, countless people prayed to Martin, asking him for his prayers. His feast day is November 11.

Check any calendar with liturgical information on it, and you will see that each month is checkered with the names of saints whose feast days fall throughout the year. Many are named as patron saints. Saint Joseph is the patron saint of workers. Saint Anthony is the saint to ask for help if you lose something. Saint Jude is the patron saint of hopeless situations. Saint Francis of Assisi is the patron saint of animals and ecology. Saint Matthew is the patron saint of accountants and bankers, and Saint Thérèse of Lisieux is the patron saint of missionaries and florists. People with eye trouble should pray to Saint Lucy, and teenagers should ask Saint Aloysius Gonzaga to pray for them. . . .

The list is very long, and the point of it all is both grand and simple: that we belong to a community that transcends time and space, a community that includes people both in this world and the next. Just as we pray for one another in this world, our saint-friends in the next world can pray for us, as well. It's that simple, and it's that delightful. The traditional term for all this is "the communion of saints."

To repeat: Catholics do not worship saints, and we do not worship the Blessed Mother. We worship only God. We *venerate* Mary and the saints, and we cultivate devotion to them much as we cultivate a "devotion" to anyone we love. Our devotions to Mary and the saints serve this purpose and this purpose alone. To pray to a saint is to address oneself to the power and grace of God active in a person who now enjoys eternal life. Period.

One of the most popular traditional devotions is called a "novena." The term *novena* comes from the Latin word for "nine," because a novena takes nine days to complete. When someone makes a novena to Saint Anthony or Saint Jude, for example, the person says prayers to Saint Anthony or Saint Jude each day for nine days, asking the saint to join in prayer for a particular intention.

There is nothing magical about praying for nine days. This is simply a way to respond to the admonition of Jesus to be persistent in prayer and "to not lose heart" (Luke 18:1). When you think about it, to pray a prayer for nine days consecutively does take persistence; you have to work at not losing heart. It's a wonderful tradition, when you think about it.

Every Catholic life is deeper, stronger, and richer when it includes a devotional component in its spirituality. Catholicism is a particular blessing in this respect because there is so much to draw upon, so many resources to take advantage of.

"The Church is the Body of Christ. Through the Spirit and his action in the sacraments, above all the Eucharist, Christ, who once was dead and is now risen, establishes the community of believers as his own Body."

Catechism of the Catholic Church
(no. 805)

Church People and Church Leaders

Catholicism has several unique characteristics, but two of them are of particular interest in this chapter. (We will discuss them all in the last chapter.) The first is Catholic sacramentalism, which we already mentioned in an earlier chapter; the church's perception that all of creation reflects and manifests the presence of its Creator. The second is its universality, its openness and adaptability to virtually any human culture and society. As Father Richard McBrien explains in *Catholicism:* "The word *Catholic* is derived from the Greek adjective, *katholikos*, meaning 'universal,' and from the adverbial phrase, *kath' holou,* meaning 'on the whole.'"

Catholicism welcomes the good, the true, and the beautiful—no matter what their source—and one reason it is able to do this is its hierarchical structure. Rooted in developments in the earliest years of the Christian community, the first indications of which are clearly present in the New Testament, the church's leadership structure helps the church, as a whole, remain faithful to the message and mission of Jesus, and to its sacramentality, regardless of country, culture, or historical situation. The papacy serves as a focal point of unity, and each individual pope does his best to keep the church, the people of God, faithful to the gospel and to its own deepest and most sacred traditions.

If we didn't have the papacy it would be easy for the Catholic Church in various countries and cultures to wander off on its own and become something distinct from the "one, holy, catholic, and apostolic" church. This traditional description of the church simply means that the church is characterized by unity ("one"), is in spite of its human imperfections a source of God's self-gift or grace ("holy"), is all-encompassing ("catholic"), and traces its existence directly to the apostles of Jesus ("apostolic").

"The *Pope,* Bishop of Rome and Peter's successor," explains the *Catechism of the Catholic Church,* "is the perpetual and visible source and foundation of the unity both of the bishops and of the whole company of the faithful" (no. 882). Of course, the pope can't be involved in the details of all the different parts of the church in all the countries where it exists. Therefore, we have bishops who "are the visible source and foundation of unity in their own particular Churches" (*Catechism of the Catholic Church,* no. 886). Each bishop is in charge of a geographical area called a diocese. A large or important diocese is called an archdiocese, and its head is an archbishop. Finally, in each diocese there are a number of parishes, and typically each parish gathers around its pastor who is a priest. If a priest is not available, sometimes a parish has a lay person or permanent deacon who may be called a "pastoral administrator."

Being Catholic does not mean that we view the pope and/or the bishops as a constant source of infallible, divinely inspired information. Even the pope is not infallible, and he *teaches* infallibly only under very limited circumstances — something that has happened only once since the First Vatican Council articulated this doctrine in 1870. Being Catholic does mean that we accord the pope and the bishops and what they say deep respect. It does not mean that when the pope or a bishop issues a statement on one issue or another all further discussion is cut off, although this may be the hope of the Vatican officials who issue the document. Often it means that the discussion only then gets going in earnest.

In a popular culture that frequently models its behavior, attitudes, and beliefs on the example set by celebrities from the entertainment and sports industries, being Catholic means we take all that with more than a few grains of salt. We believe that reliable wisdom upon which to base one's life is more likely to come from Scripture and Sacred Tradition as interpreted by the pope and the bishops than from a movie star, professional athlete, or member of a rock band. Such people have glitz and glib phrases in abundance, but they rarely become successful by loving God and neighbor. Often—not always, but often—if you get close to such people they turn out to be confused, unhappy souls who made the mistake of believing their own publicity.

Scripture and Sacred Tradition are the irreplaceable sources of wisdom and guidance for Catholics. Scripture refers, of course, to the Bible, but Sacred Tradition may not be so clear. Sacred Tradition does not refer to particular customs or practices that may change. Sacred Tradition, in Father McBrien's words, is "both the process of 'handing on' the faith and that which has been handed on. Tradition . . . includes Scripture, the essential doctrines of the Church, the Eucharist and the other sacraments, and so forth."

How can Sacred Tradition include Scripture? Look at it this way. In a very real sense, Sacred Tradition is the faith community's ongoing experience of the risen Christ. This, at rock bottom, is what gave birth to the Scriptures. It is the faith experience of the community that is foundational, but Scripture serves as a kind of measuring stick for in it we find the unrepeatable experiences from which the whole rest of the church's history developed. Thus, Scripture and Sacred Tradition go together and cannot be separated because, in a sense, they are one. This is why it's easy to interpret the Bible in strange ways once a person separates himself or herself from the faith community and its ongoing experience of Sacred Tradition.

Catholicism teaches that the Bible is free from error, but not in the way fundamentalist Christian sects believe. The *Catechism of the Catholic Church* quotes from the Second Vatican Council's document on divine revelation: ". . . the books of Scripture firmly, faithfully, and without error teach *that truth which God, for the sake of our salvation,* wished to see confided to the Sacred Scriptures" (no. 107, emphasis added).

In other words, anything in the Bible that has to do with something that is unrelated to "our salvation" *may* be inconsistent with the facts. Historical and scientific information in the Bible, for example, may not stand the test of modern scientific knowledge or research. One task of the pope and bishops is to distinguish in the Bible between that which is "for the sake of our salvation" and that which is not. Interestingly enough, this never seems to have been necessary. The pope and bishops leave such matters to Scripture scholars and the common sense and discernment of the whole community of faith.

One reason the Catholic Church has survived for some two thousand years is its hierarchical structure. The pope and the bishops serve to keep the church on target, more or less. That doesn't mean that the occasional pope or bishop doesn't do something incompatible with the gospel, even outright stupid or unjust. It simply means that in the long run, through the leadership of the pope and the bishops, the Holy Spirit keeps the church from making any ultimately fatal mistakes. Indeed, the history of the church is riddled with wrongheaded choices and unfortunate behavior on the part of its leaders. What matters most, however, is that the church as a whole keeps coming back to its own deepest and purest vision.

Sometimes people become ex-Catholics because they were offended by a particular priest, or disagree with something a bishop or pope said. Sometimes people "leave the church" because they disagree with some official church teaching or pronouncement or because they were scandalized by the behavior of some official church figure or a particular parish community. This can be a perfectly understandable action, depending on the situation, but sometimes such choices are largely self-serving. Sometimes people who become ex-Catholics reveal a naive inability to deal with the real world where nothing and no one will ever measure up to their expectations or personal ideology, not even the church. Such people sometimes seem to think that unless the church is perfect, as they understand perfection, they will have nothing to do with it.

Years ago, sociologist and novelist Father Andrew M. Greeley said it well. He said that if you can find a perfect church you should go ahead and join it. But as soon as you do, it won't be perfect anymore.

There is only one way to evaluate any institution or group, and that is to take a close look at its most basic ideals and goals. If you can agree with those ideals and goals, feel attracted to them, admire them and think they are ideals and goals worth living for, that institution or group is worth joining. Unfortunately, sometimes people look not at the ideals and goals but at how well the members of the group live up to those ideals and goals. This is a mistake. If your main concern is the behavior of the people in the group, you may join a truly weird organization. You may come across a swell bunch of folks who are friendly, supportive, and open to your involvement. But they also may happen to be Nazis, or a Hell's Angels motorcycle club . . . You would want to see if you can agree with such a group's ideals and goals before you join up.

There is only one way to evaluate the Catholic Church, and that is to take a close look at its most basic ideals and ultimate goals, not at how well the members of the church live up to them. The members of the church are weak, sinful, floundering, self-centered, and frequently have their shoestrings tied together. The church as a whole will never embody perfectly the ideals and goals of its Founder. It's a church of both magnificent saints and terrible sinners, huge successes and monumental failures. Mostly, however, the church is quite ordinary people who are grateful for their faith—their relationships with the risen Christ and one another—who go about their ordinary daily lives doing the best they can. In other words, mostly the church is people like you and me.

Catholics and non-Catholics alike sometimes use "the church" to refer not to the church as a whole but to the church's leaders, particularly the pope, or the Vatican, and official church teachings. "The church says this," or "The church teaches that." This is an understandable perspective, but not one that is entirely felicitous. "The church" is all of us, the entire people who make up the church. God has willed to make people holy—"hale and hearty"—"not as individuals without any bond or link between them, but rather to make them into a people who might acknowledge him and serve him in holiness" (*Catechism of the Catholic Church*, no. 781).

We, all of us together, are the church. The pope and the bishops, all by themselves, could not be the church. The Vatican bureaucracy ("the curia"), all by itself, could not be the church. All the priests and all the members of religious orders and congregations alone could not be the church. Neither could we seekers, the laity, all by ourselves, be the church. It takes all of us together to be the church, the countless ordinary Catholics all over the world together with our leaders, local and international.

Being Catholic means participation in the life of a local faith community, a parish. It means being a prayerful person in some way that works for you, and it means every day trying to welcome the grace or self-gift of God into your life to guide and influence everything that you do. Being Catholic means, therefore, regular participation in the Mass and reception or celebration of the sacrament of Reconciliation or Forgiveness now and then, as well. Catholics also believe that the church's leaders, the pope and the bishops, present teachings that inspire and guide us along trustworthy paths, so we pay attention to those as a part of being Catholic.

At the same time, being Catholic means listening not only to the pope and the bishops but to the Catholic community as a whole. We need to hear what our fellow believers say as a community, for the Holy Spirit speaks there, too. We need to listen to one another in our parishes, and we need to pay attention to the work of Catholic writers and artists. Sometimes artists and writers provide prophetic insights, that is, insights that genuinely echo the word and will of God for our time. We should never expect the pope and the bishops to do our thinking for us. They can guide and inform, that's about it. There are countless issues in the modern world that require us to bring our faith and common sense up to speed and make the best choices we can.

One of the best ways to stay in touch with what the Holy Spirit may say through the whole community of faith is to be a regular reader of Catholic magazines, newspapers, and books. There are some "gag-me-with-a-spoon" Catholic television programs, but there are also some quality Catholic television shows, and those are worth watching. There are conservative Catholic publications, liberal Catholic publications, and many that are middle-of-the-road, and they all have something of value to offer. They can all help us to *think* about what it means to live as adult Christians and bring our faith into play in every aspect of our everyday lives, which is where it belongs.

The Holy Spirit speaks to us not only through officially sanctioned, explicitly Catholic sources. The "word of God" can come to us through a daily newspaper, a novel by a non-Catholic or non-Christian author, or a neighbor who has no formal religious connections. Much about the dominant popular culture and its media supports a worldview that is materialistic and self-centered, it's true. But sometimes the popular culture also supports values and ideals consistent with a Christian way of life. There can be a strong temptation to allow oneself to be drawn to one extreme or the other, but neither extreme is consistent with being Catholic.

It can be easy to view "the world" as evil, as if only in the church is goodness, truth, and beauty to be found. It can be easy to relegate the church to one hour a week—or every two or three weeks—while living a life dictated almost entirely by the dominant popular culture. The Catholic ideal, however, is in the middle, living with the tension of a life that is *in* the world and *involved* in the world's concerns. The Catholic ideal is to discover goodness, truth, and beauty in the world and in the dominant popular culture at every opportunity, while remaining rooted in the life and concerns of the church at the same time. It's not an easy balancing act, but it is a rewarding one, and it is the one Catholicism holds up as the ideal.

Together, Catholic leaders and Catholic people support one another in this sometimes risky project. The church's leaders are there to offer tips and guidelines, sometimes prophetic leadership, and being Catholic means taking their words to heart. If we sometimes disagree we do so sadly, with reluctance, eager for dialogue and discussion. For the church's ordinary people are the only ones, most of the time, who can carry the spirit and message of the gospel into the everyday world. That is our challenge, and that is our greatest privilege.

"In the work of teaching and applying Christian morality, the Church needs the dedication of pastors, the knowledge of theologians, and the contribution of all Christians and men of good will. Faith and the practice of the Gospel provide each person with an experience of life 'in Christ,' who enlightens him and makes him able to evaluate the divine and human realities according to the Spirit of God. Thus the Holy Spirit can use the humblest to enlighten the learned and those in the highest positions."

Catechism of the Catholic Church
(no. 2038)

Telling Right from Wrong

We live in confusing times, surrounded by many complex moral issues. Does a terminally ill person have the right to ask a physician's help to end his or her own life? Is war an acceptable way to resolve international disputes? Is abortion murder? Does anyone have the right to use even socially acceptable drugs, such as nicotine, which will likely lead to a painful early death? Is the death penalty an acceptable form of punishment? Is "living together" without being married a prudent choice? May homosexual behavior be tolerated? Can married couples use contraceptives and still be good Catholics? Is it okay for a woman whose husband is infertile to be inseminated using the sperm of an anonymous third-party donor? May a woman who is unable to carry a pregnancy to term have another woman do this for her ("surrogate motherhood")?

Many books have been written on questions such as these, and even more will be written, so we are not about to settle any of these issues in one short chapter here. In a very real sense, it's slightly out of kilter to even discuss ethical or moral issues in this book, for as Dr. Edward Stevens explains in *Making Moral Decisions* (Paulist Press, 1981), religion cannot supply all the answers to all our moral problems in today's complex ethical climate. "The fact is that human beings make moral norms," Dr. Stevens says. "Religion can preach them, claim that they are the divine will and promise rewards and punishments, but moral codes are human constructions. All we have to go on are our minds, our hearts and each other. Humans are intelligent; humans are free; humans are social. This is the basis of morality . . . "

The *Documents of Vatican II* and the *Catechism of the Catholic Church* say little about morality or ethics in general. All the same, Judaism, and later Christianity, have always tried on the basis of human reason and their ongoing experience of the Divine Mystery to perceive and articulate what is good for persons, human relationships, and the earth ("moral") and what is bad for persons, human relationships, and the earth ("immoral"). Both the Hebrew and Christian Scriptures include such prescriptions. Official church documents frequently address the perplexing moral issues of our time. Indeed, official church teachings often seem to claim divine authority, leaving little if any room for individual conscience.

In recent decades, the best example of this is the church's official prohibition on the use of artificial contraceptives. This is also the best example of a conflict between an official church teaching and what we might call the church's "common conscience." For the overwhelming majority of married Catholics in the so-called developed nations disagree with this official church teaching and, in good conscience, use artificial contraceptives. This raises yet another issue. Is it acceptable for Catholics to behave in such a manner, that is, to dissent from a solemn church teaching on a moral issue?

Moral theology includes numerous distinctions, many of which may send the average person's mind into a tailspin trying to keep track of them. But there is one basic distinction it is good to keep in mind. Dr. Edward Stevens points out that there are no absolute moral *answers*, but there *are* absolute moral *values*, and there *are* absolute moral *principles*. Thus, life is an absolute moral *value*, and "Life is to be preserved" is an absolute moral *principle*. How this value and this principle should be applied in a specific situation and set of circumstances, however, requires *answers*, and there are no answers that apply in all situations and all circumstances. Such is our fragile human condition. For example, the preservation of life is an absolute value, but if a crazed killer breaks into my home I am fully justified in taking his or her life in order to protect my own life and the lives of my spouse and children.

Most Catholics are aware that official church teachings frequently come couched in a language and style suggesting that once the official church has spoken, that should be the end of the discussion for Catholics. Yet even a bit of research shows that for Catholicism the final court of appeal is not the official teaching but the conscience of the individual person. Saint Augustine, one of the greatest theologians in the history of the church, some fifteen hundred years ago declared that even if an angel of God should appear and order you to do something contrary to your conscience, you are bound to obey your conscience.

In the mid-1870s, Cardinal John Henry Newman (1801–90), an English convert to Catholicism and one of the greatest Catholic thinkers of modern times, wrote a letter to the Duke of Norfolk. In this letter he said: "Certainly, if I am obliged to bring religion into after-dinner toasts (which indeed does not seem quite the thing) I shall drink—to the Pope, if you please—still, to conscience first, and to the Pope afterwards."

In more recent times, Pope John Paul II in his international bestseller, *Crossing the Threshold of Hope* (Knopf, 1994), restated the ancient view: "If man is admonished by his conscience—even if an erroneous conscience, but one whose voice appears to him as unquestionably true—he must always listen to it. What is not permissible is that he culpably indulge in error without trying to reach the truth."

Now a very conservative Catholic would probably interpret that last sentence to mean that "error" must always be identified with any position contrary to the official church teaching. But clearly that is not the pope's intention. To "culpably indulge in error" means to refuse to consider the church's official teaching at all, not to mention other points of view, and cling to one's own narrow perspective out of sheer selfish stubbornness. A constant, honest, open-minded "trying to reach the truth" is a basic characteristic of any Catholic approach to moral issues.

The *Catechism of the Catholic Church* is clear on this question, insisting, first, that we must

do all we can to have a "well-formed conscience," one which "formulates its judgments
according to reason, in conformity with the
true good willed by the wisdom of the Creator." Indeed, everyone "must avail himself of
the means to form his conscience" (no. 1798).
Ultimately, however, "A human being must
always obey the certain judgment of his conscience" (no. 1800).

To deny this perspective may lead to a kind
of emotional security unattainable any other
way, but this kind of security may not be
entirely compatible with authentic Christian
faith. It can be quite comfortable to say, well,
when the official church speaks God speaks,
and that means we don't have to puzzle over
what's right and what's wrong. To adopt this
position, however, may be symptomatic of an
attitude bordering on idolatry. The church's
human institutions, including its official teaching authorities, are not God, they are fallible
human beings—open to the Holy Spirit in what
they say, before they say it, we hope, but fallible
all the same. They are, to be sure, in a special
place in the community of faith, and their words
should be taken far more seriously than what
you read in the newspapers. But in the end it is
possible to be a good Catholic and still disagree
with a non-infallible official church teaching,
which virtually all church teachings are.

The Holy Spirit works through the papacy, the episcopacy (that is, the bishops), and other church institutions, but to make an absolute identification of the Holy Spirit with every word of every official church teaching is naive and unrealistic. Nothing in Scripture, Sacred Tradition, or official church teachings suggests that the Holy Spirit guarantees to cancel all human imperfections, blind spots, and short-sightedness whenever the human beings who produce official church teachings decide to do so.

There is a temptation toward "creeping infalliblism." Under certain strictly limited conditions the pope may teach infallibly, but this does not mean that we should take every teaching that issues from the Vatican as virtually infallible. Yes, official church teachings should carry far more authority and influence than, say, media celebrities. But official church teachers do not have a full and infallible grasp of the mind of God at all times and in all places. We may not act as if they do and abandon our own conscience and the need to "work out your own salvation with fear and trembling" (Philippians 2:12).

Bottom line: being Catholic means to accept responsibility for your own life and choices before God. There are absolute values and absolute principles, but there are no absolute answers. The right thing to do in one situation may not be the right thing to do in another, and ultimately we must follow our conscience. This does not mean that we are without practical tools, however. There is a process anyone can use to make responsible decisions, and it means answering a series of five questions and then taking three steps:

1. What is the question or dilemma?

Let's take one of the most common issues that face young adult Catholics today, the issue of cohabitation. "Shall we live together without being married?"

2. What are the alternatives?

The alternatives are easy to identify. Either we can live together or not live together.

3. What people will my/our decision affect?

This is a critical question that will not receive much support from the popular culture where individualism is rampant. As far as the dominant popular culture is concerned what I or we, as a couple, do is nobody else's business, not even the other members of my immediate family. If I'm a young adult, my parents and the rest of the adult community should butt out and not give me any grief about any of the choices I make.

From a Catholic perspective, however, our family and wider community relationships cannot be separated from our relationship with

God. If I make a choice that harms my relationship with family, friends, and the wider community, that choice has a direct impact on the quality of my relationship with the Creator of the universe. If our choice to "live together" will cause anguish or scandal to our extended family and members of our church community, then it is not a minor concern—not minor at all.

It's necessary to ask, in particular, about the impact of my choice on the wider community. If I choose to cohabit with a person to whom I am not married, how will that affect the fabric of life in society at large? Will it strengthen the web of society if we live together without a permanent and public commitment not only to ourselves but to society, a promise that for our sake and for the sake of society we will stay together as long as we both shall live? Or will this have no impact on society at all?

4. What will be the consequences of my decision for myself and others?

There may seem to be no consequences to myself or others should I decide to live with someone to whom I am not married. A good question to ask is, "Why did the tradition of not living together before marriage develop in the first place?" Was it merely the result of the hang-ups of earlier generations, or were there perhaps some valid and healthy reasons? If we live together will we feel more free or less free to make a final decision about marriage?

"Living together" almost always includes full sexual intimacy. How do I really, honestly feel about this? What will the consequences be on an emotional level for both of us? What if a pregnancy should result—"accidents" do happen—before we decide about marriage?

5. What would Jesus have me do?

For anyone who takes his or her faith seriously, prayer will be an important part of the decision-making process because prayer is already a part of his or her daily life. "Prayer" is not the same for everyone. For some, prayer happens at set times, at the beginning and end of the day, for example. For others, prayer is more an informal running conversation with God that goes on at irregular times throughout the day. In either case, the idea is to consciously include God in one's everyday life, that is, to be open to the influence of the Holy Spirit in all of one's activities. So when a particularly important choice must be made, it's not as if the God I include in the process is Someone new to me.

Still, this particular choice probably grabs my attention with special intensity. So my prayer may be something like this: "Lord Jesus, help me to see the right thing to do in this situation.

Should we live together or not? What's best for each of us and for our relationship? Help me to see the light."

6. Consult some "higher authorities."

Making a good decision can be a humbling experience. We may have to admit that, just possibly, we do not have all the information we need to make a good choice. Frequently the inclination is to go with whatever information and attitudes we have assimilated from the dominant popular culture, from friends and acquaintances, from the mass media, and so forth. Much of this "information" resides in us on an unconscious level, and it surfaces to a conscious level only in the form of an assumption we are inclined to act upon, something like, "Everybody is doing it."

In order to make a good choice we need to admit that maybe we don't have all the information we need. Maybe we sense a nagging doubt that the attitudes and information we get from the dominant popular culture are the best available. Ask yourself, *"Why* do I want to cohabit? What's the point?"

Maybe we should give official church teachings—which object to cohabitation—the benefit of the doubt, at least long enough to find out why this official church prohibition exists. Maybe we should talk with a veteran married couple we know whose opinions we trust.

Maybe we should talk with a priest. Maybe we should read a book on the topic. Maybe we should look into some research that has been done on the phenomenon of cohabitation which, after all, has only become common in the last generation or so. What about civil law? How does it affect cohabiting couples? What if you decide while cohabiting to buy a house, a car, or some furniture? Who has legal ownership should you decide to separate? "Living together" may not be as simple as it sounds . . .

7. Make a decision and trust in God.

Once you clearly articulate the question or dilemma facing you; once you line up all the alternatives; once you understand the people upon whom your decision will have an impact and the consequences of your decision for yourself and others; once you pray about your decision and consult "higher authorities," then you must decide. Sooner or later, once you go through all the steps in the decision-making process, even if you're still not sure, you have no choice but to make a choice. Your decision may be to not make a decision right now, but that, too, is a decision with consequences.

Regardless of your decision, you stand spiritually naked before God and say, "This is the decision I have decided to make. I'm making the best decision I can with the information I have. No one is responsible for this decision except me, and I accept the consequences of this decision regardless of what they may be. If the consequences are pleasant, great. If the consequences are unpleasant, I can't blame my parents, my teachers, society, or anyone else. I make the choice, and I am responsible for the consequences."

8. Reevaluate.

No matter what decision you made, about cohabitation or anything else, almost always at a later time you can decide to reevaluate. You can say, "I think I had better think it out again." You can change your mind. So feel free to do so. Few decisions cannot be changed. Rejoice in the freedom of the children of God and make a different decision.

When it comes to telling right from wrong, being Catholic includes the conviction that the church's scriptures, living tradition, and official teachings are usually more trustworthy and more in touch with the human heart than what you're likely to get from much of the dominant popular culture — movies, television, magazines, the "everybody's doing it" level of information. At the same time, no one but you can make a moral decision. You can't shift that responsibility to anyone else, not even "the church."

One of the greatest writers of fiction of the twentieth century was also a Catholic who, like most Catholics, had mixed feelings about the church. His name was Graham Greene, and one of his novels is *The Heart of the Matter.* Near the end of the story, Scobie, the main character, takes his own life. Scobie's wife, Helen, meets with Father Rank, the parish priest, and declares that Scobie was "a bad Catholic."

> "That's the silliest phrase in common use," Father Rank said.
>
> "And at the end of this—horror. He must have known that he was damning himself," [Helen Scobie said.]
>
> "Yes, he knew that all right. He never had any trust in mercy—except for other people."
>
> "It's no good even praying. . . ."
>
> "Father Rank . . . said furiously, "For goodness sake, Mrs. Scobie, don't imagine you—or I—know a thing about God's mercy."
>
> "The Church says . . ."
>
> "I know the Church says. The Church knows all the rules. But it doesn't know what goes on in a single human heart."

Being Catholic means to stay open in all good will to what "the church says." But it also means to keep in mind the words of Father

Rank. For all its virtues and all the blessings it brings, the church "doesn't know what goes on in a single human heart."

Ultimately, we're on our own. But God's love is absolutely reliable.

"Coming to see in the faith their new dignity, Christians are called to lead henceforth a life 'worthy of the gospel of Christ' [Philippians 1:27]. They are made capable of doing so by the grace of Christ and the gifts of his Spirit, which they receive through the sacraments and through prayer."

Catechism of the Catholic Church
(no. 1692)

Being Catholic
An Overview

It should be evident by now that being Catholic is not like belonging to a club of some kind, a group one may join now and then or even regularly, an organization you merely count among the various social or hobby-oriented aspects of your life. Being Catholic is no hobby. Rather, being Catholic strikes at the roots of one's existence. As Father Richard McBrien explains in *Catholicism*, being Catholic is a way of life—indeed, it *is* life. (This chapter relies for its basic outline on Father McBrien's response to the question, "What is Catholicism?" Occasionally an idea is borrowed from Father McBrien, but for the most part the content is entirely the author's.)

Being Catholic means being rooted in a living Christian tradition, one that began some two thousand years ago and continues down to the present day. Being Catholic means dedicating oneself to a particular way of life based on the Good News of Jesus the Christ, the active presence of the risen Christ in the world, and the living traditions of Catholicism. Being Catholic means participation in a community of faith.

Being Catholic is a way to go about the project of being a person. A Catholic who takes his or her faith to heart draws first of all upon the risen Christ present in the community of faith for meaning and purpose—the traditions, values, and goals of Catholicism are central to his or her daily life. A Catholic, for example, is a disciple of Christ first, a citizen of a particular nation second. Being Catholic means making the sign of the cross first, saluting the flag second. If one's national citizenship comes into conflict with one's Christian identity, a Catholic's religious identity takes priority.

This does not mean that Catholics are automatically bad citizens; rather, it means that they gauge their citizenship according to their deepest values and ideals, those of their Catholic faith. Being Catholic does not include the desire to impose our religion on others, but it does mean that when something surfaces in the wider society that clashes with our deepest convictions about the dignity of human beings or the meaning and purpose of life, we will not remain silent.

At the same time, it is perfectly possible for Catholics to end up on various sides of political issues. Catholics may sympathize more with one political party than with another. Catholics may be political liberals or conservatives. But their ultimate ideals come from their faith, not from a specific political philosophy.

Being a Catholic is a specific way to be a Christian. Historically, Catholicism is the oldest form of Christian tradition, one that traces its existence in a direct line back to the apostles of Jesus with no breaks or interruptions. This is not to say that the Catholic Church at various times has not been unfaithful to the gospel, but eventually it always returns to the truth entrusted to it by Christ. (Orthodox traditions such as the Eastern and Russian Orthodox churches can make a similar claim, but we don't have the space to discuss this here. Any good volume of church history will explain it for you.)

Catholicism has seven characteristics that distinguish it, in particular, from mainline Protestant and sectarian Christian churches:

1. Catholicism is sacramental.

Being Catholic means "seeing" the Divine Mystery present in created realities, things one can see, taste, smell, touch, and feel. Being

Catholic means perceiving the infinite in the finite, the divine in the human, spiritual things in material things. Being Catholic means blinking one's eyes in joyful amazement at finding the spiritual in the material, the Most High God in the ordinary. Being Catholic means finding eternal realities in everyday things. Being Catholic includes the delightful perception that everything God created is sacred.

Because Catholicism finds created realities to be sacred realities, it is no great leap to encounter the risen Christ in the seven official sacraments of the church: Baptism, Confirmation, Eucharist, Reconciliation, Marriage, Holy Orders, and Anointing of the Sick. When others claim to have no difficulty finding God everywhere, it puzzles Catholics when they also object to finding the Divine Mystery in specific places—bread and wine, for example, in the words of forgiveness spoken by a priest, or in the committed love of a married couple.

2. Catholicism actually *causes* the Divine Mystery to be present.

Closely related to the sacramentality of Catholicism is the fact that Catholicism, primarily through the seven sacraments, actually *causes* the Divine Mystery to have an impact on those who receive the sacraments. Catholicism carries and gives the real presence of the Divine Mystery—the Risen Christ—to its members. This happens not just inwardly, on a subjective level, but objectively, in various observable events such as the Eucharist and the other sacraments.

In other words, God is not just present for Catholics as the invisible, totally transcendent object of belief or faith. Rather, God is also imminent, here, present and accounted for. Therefore being Catholic means encountering the risen Christ in and through the church and its sacraments. This encounter does not happen merely in the subjective interiority of the person, it happens objectively, "out there," in the world, in time and space, in an observable fashion.

Sacraments are not magic, mind you. We do not control God by pronouncing the "right" words and performing the "right" actions. Rather, the risen Christ makes a gift of himself in and through the church—which is all of us—at all times, and in seven special situations we are able, through the freely given grace of God, to be present to this gift.

The role of the ordained priest takes on added importance for Catholics because the priest is the one specifically designated at special times to focus the presence of the risen Christ for a distinct purpose in a distinct situation. Being Catholic does not mean needing a priest in order to find God present in the world or in oneself. By no means. But being Catholic does mean that there are special moments—the celebration of the sacraments—when a priest is required as a "stand-in," as it were, for the one Mediator between God and human beings, the risen Christ.

3. Catholicism is communal.

For Catholicism there is no such thing as a private relationship between the individual and God. Rather, even when the individual is in solitude the risen Christ comes by way of the community, and each individual relates to Christ as a member of that community. Many Christian sects teach that the individual has a private, personal relationship with God or with Jesus Christ that begins with and is nourished by reading and praying with the Bible. Hence the sectarian admonition, "Accept Jesus Christ as your personal savior."

For Catholicism, on the contrary, the Bible came from the community of faith, the church, and we can understand the Bible only in the context of the community from which it came. Thus, it is a distortion of the very nature of Scripture if a person attempts to interpret the Bible in isolation from the community of faith and the Sacred Tradition that gave birth to the Bible in the first place. More about this in the next section. . .

This does not mean that a person may not read Scripture in solitude, or pray in solitude.

It simply means that even when we are alone we are never alone. Even in solitude we are with the community of faith, the church, and Christ comes to us through that community. Even someone called to a life of prayer and solitude as a hermit is always in communion with the worldwide community of faith.

But Catholicism's vision of the community is not confined even by time and space. Being Catholic means membership in a community that goes beyond this world. The traditional term for this is "the communion of saints." We belong to a community that exists in both time and eternity. This is why, for example, we pray for one another in this world, but we also ask those who have passed through death into eternal life to pray for us, as well. We ask the saints to pray for us, of course. But we may also ask departed loved ones to pray for us because we all continue to participate in the life of the one community of faith that is both in and beyond time and space.

Being Catholic means to accept the ancient Christian mystery that the church, the community of faith, is the first and most basic "sacrament" of Christ's presence in our midst. The faith community of the church is, in the words of Saint Paul, the body of Christ. Thus: "Now you [plural "you"] are the body of Christ and individually members of it" (1 Corinthians 12:27).

This is why Catholicism places so much emphasis on the insight that the church, the community, is where we encounter the risen Christ through sacraments, various ministries, and institutions such as the papacy, the bishops, and church councils.

4. Catholicism is a tradition.

Being Catholic means, above all, participation in the Catholic faith community's ongoing experience of the risen Christ. This ongoing experience, and its many expressions or manifestations—from the beginning of the church down to the present—is what this living tradition is about. This experience, this living tradition, is the source of everything else that constitutes Catholicism. It was this experience that gave rise to the New Testament, documents that reflect the community's unrepeatable foundational faith experiences. This is why being Catholic means being rooted in Scripture and Sacred Tradition, for the two cannot be separated, the former comes from the latter.

The church—a collection of faith communities—existed before the collection of writings we call the New Testament. Stories were told, letters and sermons were written, people gathered to celebrate the Eucharist, and gradually the communities gave the stories a written form. Eventually, all the documents were collected together to make the New Testament. But these documents came from and are meant to nourish the tradition, the life of the community and its ongoing experience of the risen Christ.

5. Catholicism celebrates the human intellect.

Being Catholic includes a high degree of discomfort with the idea of "blind faith." Being Catholic never means shutting off the human intellect or reason. Rather, Catholicism finds faith and reason to be perfectly compatible. The human intellect will never be able to fully grasp the mystery of Christ, the church, and faith, but neither will the human intellect ever be able to fully grasp the mystery of one person's love for another.

For Catholicism, everything God created is touched by God's self-gift or grace, and that includes the human intellect. Yes, everything, including human reason, is "fallen," but everything is also "redeemed" by Christ, including the human intellect. Thus, being Catholic means more than reading the Bible and paying respectful attention to official church documents. It means reading the Bible and official church documents with one's brain and critical faculties engaged. Being Catholic means it is not acceptable to shut off one's intellect, then read the Bible and the official teachings of the church and "do what we're told to do." God gives us intellect and conscience, and we're expected to use them honestly, prayerfully, and to the best of our ability.

Being Catholic means doing a spiritual balancing act. We don't believe that reason alone can comprehend the mysteries of faith. But at the same time, we don't believe that "blind faith," divorced from the intellect, is an acceptable way to be a follower of Christ. Catholicism is not an either/or religion, it's a both/and religion. Faith *and* reason, that's the fully human way to live one's faith.

6. Catholicism finds God reflected everywhere.

Being Catholic means using one's intellect to better understand one's faith. But it also means using one's intellect to see life and all of God's creation as a reminder of God's unconditional love. Being Catholic means seeing the similarities that exist between God and the creation. God is like a sunset, God's love is like the love one finds in a good marriage, God is like a teenage girl or boy, God is like an ocean, God is like a playful puppy, God is like a hurricane . . . For Catholicism, analogies for God are endless because Catholicism emphasizes the similarities between the divine and the human, between God and the created order, between God and our own human experience.

Above all, of course, being Catholic means knowing God through the humanity of Jesus the Christ. Jesus is, you might say, the ultimate "analogy" or "metaphor" for God, to the point that he is both fully human and fully divine. Jesus is, literally, what he stands for, and no mere metaphor or analogy. Through the humanity of Jesus we learn both what God is like and what we are called to become, and will become, in the fullness of our humanity.

7. Catholicism is universal.

Being Catholic means being open to goodness, truth, and beauty no matter where they may be found, whether the source is explicitly Catholic or Christian, or not. A Catholic is ready to celebrate the goodness, truth, and beauty found in a symphony or a poem by an atheist. A Catholic is ready to accept the truth to be found in Buddhism or agnosticism. No problem.

Catholicism is adaptable, that's why you will find Catholicism in all kinds of cultural contexts. There are Hispanic Catholics, Irish Catholics, Japanese Catholics, French and German Catholics, Polish Catholics, African Catholics and African-American Catholics. There are Chinese Catholics and Spanish Catholics. . . The list goes on and on.

Being Catholic means being open to a multiplicity of theological and philosophical

perspectives, so a Catholic is ready to appreciate the work of a Jewish theologian, a Protestant theologian, or an agnostic philosopher.
Being Catholic means making room for a vari-
ety of spiritualities, too. Catholics appreciate
the insights of Saint Ignatius Loyola, Saint
Dominic, and Saint Francis of Assisi. Catholicism also is open to insights from psychology,
sociology, history, and all the sciences. In a
sense, they can all be sources of "divine revelation." A novel by a writer antagonistic to religion may yield truth as easily as a novel by a
"practicing Catholic." A newspaper comic strip
may echo the gospel, and a song by a popular
singer may do the same.

In other words, to come full circle: Catholicism is *catholic,* which means universal. Look at
it this way: "narrow-minded Catholic" is an
oxymoron of gargantuan proportions.

Why Be Catholic?

Now that we are at the end of our informal seeker's guide to being Catholic, there remains one question—and a glaring one—that we have not addressed. Why be Catholic? This is a question with many possible answers, some highly technical theologically. Instead, this brief Afterword will take a more everyday approach.

Why be Catholic? Throwing caution aside, one may suggest that a person may be Catholic because—dare one say it?—being Catholic is more fun. Rigidly conservative Catholics may be shocked and scandalized by such a statement. But here is the point: as Father Andrew Greeley suggested in an article published in the *New York Times Magazine* (10 July 1994), Catholicism has great stories, and stories are the best way human beings have to explain

161

reality. Stories are the best way we have to make sense out of life.

Of course, if you wish you can line up a whole regiment of reasons not to be Catholic. Father Greeley ticks them off quick-time: The church is too authoritarian, discriminates against women and homosexuals, and tries to control the behavior of married couples in the bedroom. Church leaders try to impose the Catholic position regarding abortion on everyone else. Church leaders squash dissent and disagreement whenever they can. The Vatican can't seem to see straight when it comes to sex. The pope opposes birth control in countries where the population increases by leaps and bounds. Catholics are often embarrassed by their local bishops when they hold forth on social policies. Some bishops and priests are insensitive and controlling. Lay people have no say in how their contributions are spent. Many priests are unhappy and leave to marry the first chance they get. Church leaders have tried to hide sexual abuse by priests, and now it pays out millions of dollars to compensate those hurt by priests who were supposed to be celibate. At the same time, church leaders apparently want to make married couples feel guilty about enjoying sexual pleasure.

Father Greeley adds that quite often such criticisms are unfair and inaccurate. Surveys indicate, for example, that most priests are among the happiest people you are likely to find. The church was organized on democratic principles for the first thousand years of its existence, and it could be so organized again. And so forth. . . Regardless, if someone is looking for a reason to not be Catholic, or to "leave the church," he or she will find reasons satisfactory to him or her without much trouble.

All the same, most Catholics remain Catholic. They remain Catholic because they *like* being Catholic. Father Greeley refers to research data from Michael Hout, of the Survey Research Center at the University of California at Berkeley, which shows that for the past thirty years, at least, the Catholic defection rate has remained steady at 15 percent. Half of those who leave the church do so after marriage to someone from another tradition whose religious convictions are stronger than those of the formerly Catholic spouse. The other half who leave do so for other reasons such as anger at church authorities or disagreement about church teachings on sexually-related topics. This means that 85 percent of all Catholics remain Catholic.

Most Catholics remain Catholic because Catholicism has so many wonderful stories, and Catholicism has wonderful stories because of its sacramentalism, which we discussed in the main part of this book. Catholics find God, the

Divine Mystery, the love that moves the stars and the other planets, in what Father Greeley calls "the objects and events and persons of ordinary life." Therefore, we have stories about angels and saints, we have stories about souls in purgatory, and we have stories about Mary, the Blessed Mother. Catholicism has, to quote Father Greeley again, "stained glass windows and statues and stations of the cross and rosaries and medals and the whole panoply of images and devotions that were so offensive to the austere leaders of the Reformation."

Above all, of course, we have the story, true as it can be, of Jesus who is God's own Son, who came into the world as a helpless infant, lived with a human mother and father, gathered some disciples, taught that God's love has no limits and we should therefore stop being afraid, was killed horribly for his trouble, and was raised by God on the third day to remain with his people for as long as time shall last.

Catholicism offers poetry, metaphors, and analogies—all of which keep us in touch with God's love—and organizes them into a way of life, a way of life marked by the great festivals and feasts of the liturgical year, a way of life that discovers God everywhere. All this adds up to something 85 percent of the people who are born into Catholicism wouldn't give up for anything or anyone. No way.

Father Greeley retells a delightful old Catholic story that sums it all up rather well. It seems that one day Jesus decided to stroll around heaven to see how things were going. He couldn't help but see that there were some people in heaven who, he was sure, did not belong there, at least not until they had put in a good long time in purgatory. Jesus was not pleased, so he marched right out to the Pearly Gates where he confronted Saint Peter. Jesus demanded that Saint Peter account for all the people in heaven who should not be there. Saint Peter insisted that it was not his fault. Who then? Jesus demanded. Well, Peter replied, you're not going to like this, but when I turn them away from the front gate here, they go around to the back door and your mother lets them in!

The "feel" behind this story for what's going on in life, the world, the universe, and after death, is as Catholic as it can be. It is this "feel" that most Catholics find so attractive, and this is a perfectly wonderful reason for being Catholic.

Of course, Catholicism does not ignore the presence of darkness and death, cruelty and sin in the world. Catholicism faces such realities squarely and struggles with them. In the long run, Catholicism says, suffering, cruelty, and death are not and never will be victorious. We face darkness, suffering, and sin because Jesus faced them and lived through them, and died, just as we will. Just as death and suffering did not triumph over Jesus, neither will they triumph over us.

Why be Catholic? There are many reasons of a theological and historical nature. We could talk for hours about the Catholic Church being the original Christian community that goes back in an uninterrupted line to Jesus and his disciples. We could talk about finding in the Catholic Church the potential for the fullest manifestation of God's self-gift, or grace, in the world. But for most people, on a daily basis, this line of discussion may fall flat.

What matters is what Catholicism offers people in the weave of their everyday lives. What Catholicism offers is a sensibility, a perception that God's love is closer to us than we are to ourselves, and Catholicism offers a cornucopia of stories, and sacraments, and customs, and traditions, that keep this sensibility alive. All this is true in the midst of the ordinary, in the midst of joyful times, and even in the midst of suffering and death.

Why be Catholic? Because Catholicism has great stories and has more of them. Moreover, who among us wouldn't jump at the chance to have Jesus' mother let us in by the back door?

Index